The Original
Summer Bridge Activities™

GRADES 7 to 8

Teacher Recommended!

Carson-Dellosa Publishing LLC
P.O. Box 35665 • Greensboro, NC 27425 USA

carsondellosa.com

Caution: Exercise activities may require adult supervision. Before beginning any exercise activity, consult a physician. Written parental permission is suggested for those using this book in group situations. Children should always warm up prior to beginning any exercise activity and should stop immediately if they feel any discomfort during exercise.

Caution: Before beginning any food activity, ask parents' permission and inquire about the child's food allergies and religious or other food restrictions.

Caution: Nature activities may require adult supervision. Before beginning any nature activity, ask parents' permission and inquire about the child's plant and animal allergies. Remind the child not to touch plants or animals during the activity without adult supervision.

The authors and publisher are not responsible or liable for any injury that may result from performing the exercises or activities in this book.

ISBN 978-1-62057-614-4

04-055141151

Table of Contents

About Summer Learning

Dear Parents:

Did you know that many children experience learning loss when they do not engage in educational activities during the summer? This means that some of what they have spent time learning over the preceding school year evaporates during the summer months. However, summer learning loss is something that you can help prevent. Below are a few suggestions for fun and engaging activities that can help children maintain and grow their academic skills during the summer.

- Read with your child every day. Visit your local library together and select books on subjects that interest your child.

- Ask your child's teacher to recommend books for summer reading.

- Explore parks, nature preserves, museums, and cultural centers.

- Consider every day as a day full of teachable moments. Measuring ingredients for recipes and reviewing maps before a car trip are ways to learn or reinforce skills.

- Each day, set goals for your child to accomplish. For example, complete five math problems or read one section or chapter in a book.

- Encourage your child to complete the activities in books such as Summer Bridge Activities™ to help bridge the summer learning gap.

To learn more about summer learning loss and summer learning programs, visit *www.summerlearning.org.*

Have a memorable summer!

Brenda McLaughlin and Sarah Pitcock
National Summer Learning Association

About Summer Bridge Activities™

Summer Bridge Activities™: Bridging Grades Seventh to Eighth helps prepare your rising eighth grader for a successful school year. The activities in this book are designed to review the skills that your child mastered in seventh grade, preview the skills that he or she will learn in eighth grade, and help prevent summer learning loss. No matter how wonderful your child's classroom experiences are, your involvement outside of the classroom is crucial to his or her academic success. Together with *Summer Bridge Activities™: Bridging Grades Seventh to Eighth*, you can fill the summer months with learning experiences that will deepen and enrich your child's knowledge and prepare your child for the upcoming school year.

Summer Bridge Activities™ is the original workbook series developed to help parents support their children academically during the summer months. While many other summer workbook series are available, Summer Bridge Activities™ continues to be the series that teachers recommend most.

The three sections in this workbook correspond to the three months of traditional summer vacation. Each section begins with a goal-setting activity, a word list, and information about the fitness and character development activities located throughout the section.

To achieve maximum results, your child should complete two activity pages each day. Each activity page is numbered by day, and activities cover a range of subjects, including reading comprehension, writing, grammar, algebra, geometry, social studies, science, and fitness. These grade-appropriate activities are presented in a fun and creative way to challenge and engage your child.

Bonus extension activities that encourage outdoor learning, science experiments, and social studies exercises are located at the end of each section. Complete these activities with your child throughout each month as time allows.

An answer key located at the end of the book allows you to check your child's work. The included flash cards help reinforce basic skills, and a certificate of completion will help you and your child celebrate his or her summer learning success!

Skills Matrix

Day	Addition & Subtraction	Algebra	Character Development	Critical Thinking	Data Analysis & Probability	Decimals, Fractions & Percentages	Fitness	Geometry & Measurement	Grammar	Language Arts	Literary Terms	Multiplication & Division	Parts of Speech	Problem Solving	Reading Comprehension	Science	Social Studies	Vocabulary	Writing
1	★			★					★			★				★			
2	★												★		★			★	
3												★	★		★				
4						★							★					★	★
5						★	★		★									★	
6						★			★						★				
7				★		★			★									★	
8						★			★		★								
9						★			★						★				
10			★			★			★		★								
11						★				★			★				★		
12									★				★	★					★
13		★		★									★						
14		★											★		★				★
15		★					★				★		★						
16		★											★		★				
17		★									★		★			★			
18		★									★		★		★				
19											★		★		★				
20		★									★		★						★
BONUS PAGES!					★											★			★
1		★											★			★		★	
2		★											★		★				
3		★											★		★			★	
4		★					★		★									★	
5		★							★						★				
6		★		★					★										★
7				★		★					★		★						
8													★	★	★				
9			★			★							★					★	
10								★					★			★		★	
11								★	★						★				

Skills Matrix

Day	Addition & Subtraction	Algebra	Character Development	Critical Thinking	Data Analysis & Probability	Decimals, Fractions, & Percentages	Fitness	Geometry & Measurement	Grammar	Language Arts	Literary Terms	Multiplication & Division	Parts of Speech	Problem Solving	Reading Comprehension	Science	Social Studies	Vocabulary	Writing
12								★					★		★				★
13						★		★					★						★
14								★	★						★				
15								★			★		★			★			
16								★	★						★		★		
17								★					★		★				
18								★			★		★			★			
19								★		★			★						★
20								★	★						★				
BONUS PAGES!								★								★	★		★
1								★	★			★						★	
2				★				★	★										★
3								★	★						★				
4							★	★	★									★	
5								★	★	★						★			
6								★	★						★				
7								★	★						★		★		
8								★	★									★	★
9								★	★						★				
10								★	★		★					★			
11								★	★						★				
12								★	★						★				
13			★					★	★							★			
14								★	★		★					★			
15								★	★						★				
16		★							★						★		★		
17				★			★		★	★									
18				★					★						★				
19				★					★	★						★			
20				★	★				★									★	
BONUS PAGES!						★											★	★	

Encouraging Summer Reading

Literacy is the single most important skill that your child needs to be successful in school. The following list includes ideas that you can use to help your child discover the great adventures of reading.

- Establish a time for reading each day. Ask your child about what he or she is reading. Try to relate the material to an event that is happening this summer or to another book or story.

- Let your child see you reading for enjoyment. Talk about the great things that you discover when you read.

- Create a summer reading list. Your child can choose books from the reading list (pages ix–x) or head to the library and explore the shelves. Ask your child to read a page or two from a book before choosing it. A general rule is if he or she does not know five or more words on the page, the book may be too difficult.

- Encourage the reading of newspaper and magazine articles, recipes, menus, and maps on a regular basis to show your child the importance of reading.

- Direct your child to books that relate to his or her interests or experiences. For example, if you are going camping, find a book about camping. This will help your child develop new interests.

- Visit the library each week. Let your child choose his or her own books, but do not hesitate to ask your librarian for suggestions. Often, librarians can recommend books based on what your child enjoyed in the past.

- Encourage your child to join a summer reading club at the library or a local bookstore. Your child may enjoy talking to friends about the books that he or she has read.

Summer Reading List

The summer reading list includes fiction and nonfiction titles. Experts recommend that students entering the eighth grade read for at least 30 minutes each day.

Decide on an amount of daily reading time for each month. You may want to write the time on the Monthly Goals page at the beginning of each section.

Fiction

Alcott, Louisa May
Little Women

Almond, David
Skellig

Avi
Crispen: The Cross of Lead

Blos, Joan W.
*A Gathering of Days: A New England
    Girl's Journal, 1830–32*

Burch, Robert
Ida Early Comes Over the Mountain

Burnford, Sheila
The Incredible Journey

Byars, Betsy
The Summer of the Swans

Clements, Andrew
Things Not Seen

Cooney, Caroline B.
The Face on the Milk Carton

Creech, Sharon
Walk Two Moons

Crew, Linda
Children of the River

Cushman, Karen
The Midwife's Apprentice
Catherine, Called Birdy

Forbes, Esther
Johnny Tremain

Funke, Cornelia
The Thief Lord

Greene, Bette
Summer of My German Soldier

Haddix, Margaret Peterson
Among the Hidden

Hiaasen, Carl
Scat

Hunt, Irene
Across Five Aprils

Lasky, Kathryn
*Dreams in the Golden Country: The Diary
    of Zipporah Feldman, a Jewish
    Immigrant Girl, New York City, 1903*

Lee, Harper
To Kill a Mockingbird

L'Engle, Madeleine
A Wrinkle in Time

Lowry, Lois
Number the Stars

Myers, Walter Dean
Somewhere in the Darkness

Summer Reading List (continued)

Fiction (continued)

O'Dell, Scott
Sing Down the Moon
Streams to the River, River to the Sea:
A Novel of Sacagawea

Paterson, Katherine
The Master Puppeteer

Paulsen, Gary
Brian's Winter
Hatchet
The Monument

Peck, Richard
A Year Down Yonder

Peck, Robert Newton
A Day No Pigs Would Die

Pullman, Philip
The Golden Compass

Rawls, Wilson
Summer of the Monkeys

Riordan, Rick
The Lightning Thief

Rushdie, Salman
Haroun and the Sea of Stories

Selznick, Brian
The Invention of Hugo Cabret

Smith, Charles R., Jr.
Rimshots: Basketball Pix, Rolls,
and Rhythms

Sperry, Armstrong
Call It Courage

Tan, Shaun
The Arrival

Taylor, Mildred D.
Roll of Thunder, Hear My Cry

Taylor, Theodore
The Cay

Twain, Mark
The Prince and the Pauper

Yates, Elizabeth
Amos Fortune, Free Man

Nonfiction

Colbert, David
Anne Frank

Curlee, Lynn
Seven Wonders of the Ancient World

Donald, Rhonda Lucas
Recycling

Hautzig, Esther
The Endless Steppe

Hecht, Jeff
Vanishing Life: The Mystery of
Mass Extinctions

Herriot, James
All Creatures Great and Small

Holtz, Lou
Winning Every Day: The Game Plan
for Success

McCullough, David
The Great Bridge: The Epic Story of the
Building of the Brooklyn Bridge

Schwager, Tina and Michele Schuerger
Gutsy Girls: Young Women Who Dare

Monthly Goals

A *goal* is something that you want to accomplish and must work toward. Sometimes, reaching a goal can be difficult.

Think of three goals to set for yourself this month. For example, you may want to exercise for 30 minutes each day. Write your goals on the lines. Post them somewhere that you will see them every day.

Draw a check mark beside each goal you meet. Feel proud that you have met your goals and continue to set new ones to challenge yourself.

1. _____

2. _____

3. _____

Word List

The following words are used in this section. Use a dictionary to look up each word that you do not know. Then, write three sentences. Use at least one word from the word list in each sentence.

appreciated	novel
auspicious	ominous
critical	perilous
foreboding	secretion
mingle	trepidation

1. _____

   _____

2. _____

   _____

3. _____

   _____

Introduction to Flexibility

This section includes fitness and character development activities that focus on flexibility. These activities are designed to get you moving and thinking about building your physical fitness and your character.

Physical Flexibility

To the average person, *flexibility* means being able to accomplish everyday physical tasks easily, such as bending to tie a shoe. These everyday tasks can be difficult for people whose muscles and joints have not been used and stretched regularly.

Proper stretching allows muscles and joints to move through their full range of motion, which is important for good flexibility. There are many ways that you stretch every day without realizing it. When you reach for a dropped pencil or a box of cereal on the top shelf, you are stretching your muscles. Flexibility is important to your health, so challenge yourself to improve your flexibility consciously. Simple stretches and activities, such as yoga and tai chi, can improve your flexibility. Set a stretching goal for the summer, such as practicing daily until you can touch your toes.

Flexibility of Character

While it is important to have a flexible body, it is also important to be mentally flexible. Being mentally flexible means being open-minded about change. It can be disappointing when things do not go your way, but this is a normal reaction. Think of a time when unforeseen circumstances ruined your recent plans. Maybe your mother had to work one weekend, and you could not go to a baseball game with friends because you needed to babysit a younger sibling. How did you deal with the situation?

A large part of being mentally flexible is realizing that there will be situations in life where unforeseen things happen. Often, it is how you react to the circumstances that affects the outcome. Arm yourself with tools to be flexible, such as having realistic expectations, brainstorming solutions to make a disappointing situation better, and looking for good things that may have resulted from the initial disappointment.

Mental flexibility can take many forms. For example, being fair, respecting the differences of other people, and being compassionate are ways that you can practice mental flexibility. In difficult situations, remind yourself to be flexible, and you will reap the benefits of this important character trait.

Solve each problem.

1. 621.75
   + 39.26

2. 68.3
   × 3.15

3. 736.2
   − 19.8

4. 35.681
   + 3.972

5. 78.8 ÷ 4 = _____

6. 96.3 ÷ 3 = _____

7. 150.5 ÷ 7 = _____

8. 8(16 − 8) = _____

9. 6(7 + 9) = _____

10. (8 − 5) × (5 + 6) = _____

Read the passage. Underline each noun. Then, draw three lines under each letter that should be capitalized.

american pioneers followed several routes on their journeys west. Pioneers from new england traveled across new york on the mohawk trail. another route led through the cumberland gap, a natural pass in the appalachian mountains that ends near the borders of kentucky, tennessee, and virginia.

the first groups of settlers crossing the appalachian mountains in the late 1700s and early 1800s followed these early trails. The popular conestoga wagon, which originated in pennsylvania and was probably introduced by mennonite german settlers, carried many pioneers migrating southward through the Great appalachian valley along the Great wagon road.

DAY I

Circle the letter next to the word that correctly completes each analogy.

11. desert : rain forest :: _____ : ravine
    A. ocean   B. canyon   C. plateau   D. mountain

12. tasteless : bland :: auspicious : _____
    A. foreboding B. favorable   C. trepidation   D. suspicious

13. sight : eyes :: touch : _____
    A. play   B. fingers   C. feel   D. move

14. bird : nest :: rabbit : _____
    A. field   B. den   C. carrot   D. burrow

15. mobile phone : battery :: human : _____
    A. food   B. clothing   C. shelter   D. shoes

Write the letter of the word from the word bank that completes each sentence.

A. cells	B. chlorophyll	C. chromosomes
D. endoplasmic reticulum	E. organelles	F. nucleus
G. interphase		

16. _____ In the first stage of cell reproduction, the _____ disappears.

17. _____ Before mitosis begins, the cell's _____ , such as chloroplast and mitochondria, make copies of themselves.

18. _____ The period of time when a cell grows and copies its DNA is called _____.

19. _____ The basic units of structure in all living organisms are the _____.

20. _____ After mitosis, each identical daughter cell has a complete set of _____.

21. _____ Plant cells use _____ to capture sunlight.

22. _____ Materials and proteins are transported through the cells by the _____.

FACTOID: The first parking meter appeared in Oklahoma on July 16, 1935.

Solve each problem.

1. 725.987 – 231.155 = _____

2. 13.58 – 7.2 = _____

3. 42.25 + 53.5 = _____

4. 432.42 – 327.89 = _____

5. 12.828 + 10.548 = _____

6. 1,343.32 – 1,032.90 = _____

7. 0.6 + 0.09 + 1.75 = _____

8. 65.78 + 54.90 = _____

9. 87.21 – 13.98 + 22.23 = _____

10. 6.77 + 0.05 = _____

A possessive noun shows ownership of the noun that follows it. Rewrite each phrase using a possessive noun.

11. the athletic shoes of the team member _____

_____

12. the breakfast of Mom _____

_____

13. the rights belonging to the students _____

_____

14. the weather found in Oakland _____

_____

15. the plans belonging to the architect _____

_____

16. the enthusiasm of the crowd _____

_____

DAY 2

Read each word. Write _P_ if the word has a positive connotation. Write _N_ if the word has a negative connotation.

17. _____ annoy

18. _____ unique

19. _____ worthless

20. _____ clumsy

21. _____ compliment

22. _____ exquisite

23. _____ glorious

24. _____ cheerful

Read the passage. Then, answer the questions.

Primary and Secondary Sources

When you conduct research for a paper, you use many sources. A primary source may be a letter, a diary, an interview, a speech, or a law. A primary source provides firsthand information about an event from the view of someone who was present when that event occurred. A secondary source, such as an encyclopedia or a textbook, is a collection and interpretation of information gathered from other sources after an event has happened. If you look at the last page in an encyclopedia entry, you may see a list of articles and books that the author consulted. A letter written home from a soldier serving in World War II is a primary source. It might tell about his experiences with other soldiers in a foreign country. A book that examines the role of the United States during World War II is a secondary source. It might discuss several soldiers' letters and draw conclusions from them.

25. What is the main idea of this passage?
    A. A textbook is a secondary source.
    B. Primary sources are written by someone who was present at an event.
    C. Research includes the use of both primary and secondary sources.

26. What kind of information do primary sources provide?_____

_____

27. What does a secondary source interpret? _____

28. Name a primary source you might use to write a research paper about the

    Klondike Gold Rush. _____

 FITNESS FLASH: Practice a V-sit. Stretch five times.

* See page ii.

Solve each problem. Round to the nearest hundredth.

1. $3.6 \div 0.3 =$ _____

2. $4.33 \div 0.3 =$ _____

3. $(1.3)(3.04)(5.46) =$ _____

4. $7.569 \div 3.459 =$ _____

5. $(4.3)(3.59) =$ _____

6. $(23.4)(3.9) =$ _____

7. $44.34 \div 32.76 =$ _____

8. $(5.5)(2.6)(4.0) =$ _____

9. $34.96 \div 3.549 =$ _____

10. $8.37 \div 4.50 =$ _____

A collective noun refers to a group, or collection, of people or things. Match each collective noun with the appropriate group.

11. _____ of locusts

12. _____ of spiders

13. _____ of stars

14. _____ of racehorses

15. _____ of information

16. _____ of elephants

17. _____ of ships

18. _____ of actors

19. _____ of events

20. _____ of dollars

21. _____ of swans

A. plague

B. herd

C. galaxy

D. fistful

E. wealth

F. bevy

G. field

H. flotilla

I. cluster

J. cast

K. chain

DAY 3

Read the passage. Then, answer the questions.

Dancing Honeybees

Many flowering plants depend on bees for pollination. When a honeybee discovers a patch of flowers with **nectar** and pollen, the bee flies to the hive to alert the other honeybees. The bee dances to communicate with the other bees in the hive.

The bee's dance is a code that explains the direction and distance of the flowers. The honeybee uses the sun as her point of reference. For example, if she performs her dance to the left of an imaginary vertical line perpendicular to the sun, this signals to the other bees that the location of the flowers is to the left of the sun. A long dance indicates a larger find, while a short dance signals a smaller discovery.

Within a short period of time, many worker bees leave the hive and head for the flowers. A honeybee can visit between 50 and 100 flowers during a single collection trip. The average honeybee produces about one-twelfth of a teaspoon of honey in her lifetime. Honeybees must visit about two million flowers to make one pound (0.45 kg) of honey.

22. Which of the following best defines the word *nectar*?
     A.   flowers where bees stop and rest
     B.   the sweet secretion from flowers
     C.   the male bee
     D.   the hive's location

23. Which of the following statements is false?
     A.   A honeybee can visit 50 to 100 flowers during a single collection trip.
     B.   Each worker bee produces about one pound (0.45 kg) of honey in a lifetime.
     C.   The length of the dance signifies how large or small the find is.
     D.   When a worker bee finds a patch of flowers, she shares the information with the other bees in the hive.

24. Which of the following best describes the setting for the passage?
     A.   anywhere in the world where bees live
     B.   western Europe, where bees originated
     C.   southern California
     D.   Vermont, whose state insect is the honeybee

FACTOID: More than 7,000 languages are spoken in the world. Some are used by only a few people.

Write >, <, or = to compare each pair of fractions.

1. $\frac{1}{2}$ ◯ $\frac{4}{8}$

2. $\frac{2}{5}$ ◯ $\frac{3}{4}$

3. $\frac{5}{6}$ ◯ $\frac{7}{8}$

4. $\frac{5}{8}$ ◯ $\frac{13}{32}$

5. $\frac{1}{8}$ ◯ $\frac{3}{5}$

6. $\frac{1}{4}$ ◯ $\frac{2}{3}$

7. $\frac{1}{6}$ ◯ $\frac{1}{3}$

8. $\frac{4}{5}$ ◯ $\frac{16}{20}$

9. $\frac{2}{3}$ ◯ $\frac{1}{2}$

Rewrite each series of fractions so that they have like denominators. Order each series from smallest to largest. Then, simplify each fraction.

Same Denominator	Smallest to Largest	Simplest Form
10. $\frac{1}{3}$, $\frac{3}{4}$, $\frac{1}{2}$		
11. $\frac{5}{6}$, $\frac{2}{9}$, $\frac{1}{3}$		
12. $\frac{1}{6}$, $\frac{7}{8}$, $\frac{3}{4}$		

A concrete noun is a person, place, or thing. An abstract noun is an idea, an emotion, or a concept. Identify the underlined noun in each sentence. Write *C* if the noun is concrete. Write *A* if the noun is abstract.

13. _____ <u>Communication</u> with others enriches our lives.

14. _____ The Statue of Liberty is often identified with <u>freedom</u>.

15. _____ We enjoy living near the <u>ocean</u>.

16. _____ At the ceremony, Matt received the Mayor's Award for the <u>bravery</u> that he demonstrated.

17. _____ Fluffy, the Carson family's <u>cat</u>, has a friendly and playful personality.

DAY 4

Use context clues to write the correct word from the word bank to complete each sentence.

| perilous | bulldozer | recipe | doze | breakfast | charcoal |

18. Of all the machines on the heavy-equipment lot, the _____ is the best to push sand and soil into a pile.

19. Because her neighbor's dog barked all night, Sarah was tired and started to _____ in her chair that morning.

20. It is _____ to chase a ball into the street when cars and other vehicles are approaching.

21. The _____ for brownies is in the striped cookbook.

22. Mrs. Frye's _____ consisted of boiled eggs and rye toast.

23. The artist used _____ to sketch the stream.

Create a new word. Write a definition for your new word. How do you pronounce it? How is it used? Write a sentence using your new word.

_____

_____

_____

_____

_____

_____

_____

_____

_____

FITNESS FLASH: Touch your toes 10 times.

* See page ii.

Solve each problem. Then, simplify each answer.

1. $\dfrac{6}{7} + \dfrac{1}{5} =$ _____

2. $\dfrac{4}{9} - \dfrac{1}{3} =$ _____

3. $\dfrac{3}{4} + \dfrac{2}{9} =$ _____

4. $\dfrac{5}{6} + \dfrac{7}{8} =$ _____

5. $\dfrac{1}{6} + \dfrac{7}{9} =$ _____

6. $\dfrac{9}{25} - \dfrac{3}{10} =$ _____

7. $\dfrac{2}{3} - \dfrac{5}{8} =$ _____

8. $\dfrac{5}{8} + \dfrac{11}{2} =$ _____

9. $\dfrac{2}{5} - \dfrac{3}{8} =$ _____

10. $\dfrac{1}{6} + \dfrac{3}{4} =$ _____

11. $\dfrac{9}{10} - \dfrac{7}{20} =$ _____

12. $\dfrac{5}{10} + \dfrac{6}{8} =$ _____

A gerund is a verb that is used as a noun. To form a gerund, add _–ing_ to the base verb. Circle the gerund in each sentence. Then, write its base verb on the line.

13. _____ A very important step is knowing what to do.

14. _____ I love hearing our band play John Philip Sousa's marches.

15. _____ When I swim, my favorite activity is floating on my back.

16. _____ Complaining never works with my parents.

17. _____ More than any other part of golf, I like putting the best.

18. _____ Going to the library with her dad was one of Shari's favorite things to do when she was a child.

DAY 5

The way a word is used in a sentence can help you determine its meaning. Read each sentence. Circle the correct meaning of each boldfaced word as it is used in the sentence.

19. That antique painting has **appreciated** over time.

   A. increased in value

   B. felt grateful for

20. A good education is **critical** for success later in life.

   A. disapproving

   B. important

21. The banker deposited $500 in the **vault**.

   A. a piece of gymnastic equipment

   B. a large safe

22. We enjoyed the **sparkling** conversation at the party.

   A. glittering

   B. interesting

23. Reyna put the horse in the **stall** after she groomed him.

   A. area of the barn

   B. halt or pause

24. Matthew thought of a **novel** approach to solving his problem.

   A. new or innovative

   B. fictional book

Hoop Twist

Have you ever watched someone swing a golf club or a baseball bat? Professional golfers and baseball players regularly work on their flexibility so that they have a broader range of motion. This allows them to hit the ball farther. Use a large hoop (or an exercise band or towel) to increase your back's range of motion. Step inside the hoop. Lift it to waist height. Hold the hoop against your back, hands spread wide apart. Gently move the hoop around your body with your hands. Your arms will twist at the shoulders from the sides of your body to the front and back. Now, move the hoop in the other direction. Keep your feet firmly planted on the floor and hips facing forward. Only your torso should move. Start slowly until you feel your muscles loosening. If using an exercise band or a towel, keep your arms in front of you and twist your torso.

CHARACTER CHECK: Think of a game you like to play. Write a TV or radio commercial promoting fairness while playing the game.

* See page ii.

Solve each problem. Simplify if possible.

1. $\dfrac{1}{8} \times \dfrac{1}{5} =$ _____

2. $\dfrac{1}{4} \times \dfrac{1}{7} =$ _____

3. $\dfrac{1}{12} \times \dfrac{1}{8} =$ _____

4. $\dfrac{3}{7} \times \dfrac{4}{5} =$ _____

5. $\dfrac{4}{5} \times \dfrac{6}{8} =$ _____

6. $\dfrac{2}{3} \times \dfrac{4}{7} =$ _____

7. $\dfrac{7}{8} \div \dfrac{3}{5} =$ _____

8. $\dfrac{9}{2} \div \dfrac{1}{3} =$ _____

9. $\dfrac{8}{3} \div \dfrac{2}{5} =$ _____

10. $\dfrac{15}{4} \div \dfrac{3}{7} =$ _____

11. $\dfrac{2}{3} \div \dfrac{3}{7} =$ _____

12. $\dfrac{3}{8} \div \dfrac{3}{4} =$ _____

A predicate nominative is a noun or pronoun that follows a linking verb and renames or describes the sentence's subject. Read each sentence. Underline the predicate nominative once. Underline the linking verb twice. Then, draw an arrow from the predicate nominative to the subject it renames.

13. *The Book Thief* by Markus Zusak is a novel for teens that is set in Germany during World War II.

14. Charles Dickens is the author of the novel, *Great Expectations*.

15. One of the main characters in J. R. R. Tolkien's book, *The Fellowship of the Ring*, is a wizard named Gandalf.

16. Homer's story, *The Iliad*, is a classic tale about the Trojan War.

17. *Harry Potter and the Sorcerer's Stone* is the first book in a series by J. K. Rowling.

18. *The Westing Game* by Ellen Raskin is a popular book.

19. *Animal Farm* and *1984* are two famous novels by George Orwell.

DAY 6

Read the passage. Then, answer the questions.

The Great Compromise

When the Founding Fathers wrote the U. S. Constitution, they debated about how many representatives each state should have in the federal government. They proposed a plan that states with larger populations should have more votes in Congress than smaller states. This was called the Virginia Plan. However, states with smaller populations disagreed with this plan. They wanted each state to have an equal number of representatives so that less-populated states would have as much say as the more populated states. Their plan was called the New Jersey Plan. After further debate, lawmakers suggested a compromise called the Connecticut Plan. The Connecticut Plan called for a bicameral legislature, or a two-house Congress. One house, called the Senate, would have the same number of representatives from each state. The other house, called the House of Representatives, would have a different number of representatives from each state, based on the state's population. The Connecticut Plan pleased both large and small states and became known as the Great Compromise.

20. Why did the less-populated states disagree with the Virginia Plan? _____

_____

_____

_____

21. Why did the more-populated states think the Virginia Plan was fair?_____

_____

22. What is a compromise? _____

23. Do you think it is important for people in government to compromise? Why or

why not?_____

_____

24. Write about a time when you had to compromise with someone. _____

_____

FACTOID: About 70 percent of Earth's species are found in just 12 countries: Australia, Brazil, China, Colombia, Ecuador, India, Indonesia, Madagascar, Mexico, Peru, and Zaire.

Solve each problem. Simplify if possible.

1. $4\frac{2}{3}$
   $+\ 3\frac{1}{2}$

2. $7\frac{5}{4}$
   $+\ 5\frac{1}{6}$

3. $6\frac{7}{8}$
   $+\ 2\frac{3}{4}$

4. $12\frac{7}{8}$
   $+\ 6\frac{1}{3}$

5. $36\frac{1}{2}$
   $+\ 25\frac{3}{10}$

6. $15\frac{5}{9}$
   $+\ 9\frac{1}{3}$

7. $6\frac{1}{4}$
   $-\ 4\frac{7}{16}$

8. $7\frac{1}{7}$
   $-\ 3\frac{6}{14}$

9. $8\frac{1}{3}$
   $-\ 2\frac{9}{15}$

A direct object is a noun or a pronoun in the predicate that receives the action of the verb. A direct object answers the question _whom_ or _what_. Circle the direct object in each sentence.

10. Every person needs an outlet for frustration.

11. Who sent me the mystery gift?

12. My mom bought a new bracelet on the Internet.

13. Joseph has recorded the minutes of the board meetings for the past 20 years.

14. Samuel Clemens portrayed life on the Mississippi River during the 1800s through the eyes of his characters, Tom Sawyer and Huckleberry Finn.

15. Should we send Kia roses for winning the district high jump competition?

16. Every student in the class enjoys Ms. Osbourne because of her wonderful sense of humor and upbeat presentations.

17. After graduating from college, Cindy plans a career in medicine.

DAY 7

Circle the letter of the correct meaning for each root word.

18. cred
    A. above
    B. believe
    C. feel

19. photo
    A. light
    B. free
    C. shape

20. morph
    A. love
    B. form
    C. change

21. alter
    A. make
    B. send
    C. other

22. port
    A. carry
    B. out
    C. in

23. script
    A. give
    B. write
    C. touch

Nick, Joey, Beki, and Carmen ran in the town's annual road race. Each person had a different jersey number (2, 13, 20, and 34) and finished in a different amount of time (10 minutes, 11 minutes, 12 minutes, and 14 minutes). Use the information and deductive reasoning to determine each person's jersey number and race time.

- The runner with the lowest jersey number also ran the slowest time.
- Nick's jersey number is 18 greater than Carmen's.
- Of the four runners, a man had the fastest finishing time.
- The sum of the digits on Beki's jersey number is 7.
- Nick finished exactly 2 minutes faster than Beki.

	2	13	20	34
Nick				
Joey				
Beki				
Carmen				

FITNESS FLASH: Do arm circles for 30 seconds.

* See page ii.

Solve each problem. Simplify if possible.

1. $5\frac{1}{3} \div 2\frac{4}{12} =$ _____

2. $7\frac{1}{2} + 6\frac{3}{4} =$ _____

3. $4\frac{4}{5} \times 3\frac{3}{4} =$ _____

4. $15\frac{3}{4} \times 3\frac{3}{7} =$ _____

5. $\frac{4}{5} \div \frac{3}{5} =$ _____

6. $5\frac{3}{5} + 8\frac{1}{4} =$ _____

7. $11\frac{1}{7} - 7\frac{5}{6} =$ _____

8. $7\frac{1}{2} - 2\frac{3}{7} =$ _____

9. $7\frac{3}{5} + 4\frac{7}{8} =$ _____

An indirect object precedes the direct object and tells *to whom* or *for whom* the action of the verb is done. It answers the question *who*. Circle the indirect object in each sentence.

10. Mr. Hanson taught the class a lesson in democracy.

11. The parts company will ship them the package by Friday.

12. If I give you the money, will you buy a T-shirt at the concert for me?

13. My dad began paying me an allowance when I was in eighth grade.

14. The Smith family prepared us a delicious meal.

15. Every student in Coach Steinman's P.E. class gave him a card or a small gift when he retired.

16. Marie Curie's radiation research earned her a Nobel Prize in 1903.

17. Our art class bought Miss Sherman a bouquet of flowers for being such a wonderful and caring teacher.

18. Bonnie showed the volunteers the donations for the canned food drive.

19. I built my brother a go-cart for the annual race.

DAY 8

An idiom is a phrase that has a different meaning than the literal meaning of each word within the expression. Underline the idiom in each sentence. Then, write what you think the idiom means.

20. When it came to political differences, Mr. Jackson drew a line in the sand.

    _____

21. Keep your shirt on! We are almost there.

    _____

22. The motor on our boat went belly up.

    _____

23. I don't see how you can keep a straight face.

    _____

24. The 100-meter dash ended in a dead heat.

    _____

25. Andrew walked through the glassware store like a bull in a china shop.

    _____

26. After spending 10 days on a beach in Hawaii, Paula returned to work and began to wade through the stack of papers on her desk.

    _____

27. During the holiday party, employees jockeyed for position to shake hands with the company president.

    _____

FACTOID: Baseball's first World Series was played in 1903 between the Boston Red Sox and the Pittsburgh Pirates.

Write each fraction as a decimal.

1. $\dfrac{4}{5}$ = _____

2. $\dfrac{3}{8}$ = _____

3. $\dfrac{3}{5}$ = _____

4. $\dfrac{9}{15}$ = _____

5. $\dfrac{17}{20}$ = _____

6. $\dfrac{1}{25}$ = _____

7. $\dfrac{9}{40}$ = _____

8. $\dfrac{18}{25}$ = _____

Write each fraction as a percentage.

9. $\dfrac{3}{4}$ = _____

10. $\dfrac{1}{4}$ = _____

11. $\dfrac{1}{2}$ = _____

12. $\dfrac{1}{10}$ = _____

13. $\dfrac{11}{100}$ = _____

14. $\dfrac{73}{100}$ = _____

15. $\dfrac{1}{5}$ = _____

16. $\dfrac{1}{20}$ = _____

Circle each direct object. Underline each indirect object.

17. John gave Wendy a necklace for Christmas.

18. Amy's parents bought her dinner at the Cold Lobster Supper Club.

19. Pablo Picasso's skills as a painter and a sculptor won him great recognition as a modern abstract artist.

20. Miguel bought his brother a new DVD for his birthday.

21. The club professional showed Juana the correct grip to use on a golf club.

22. A change in wind direction brought the Arctic explorers added trouble.

DAY 9

Read the passage. Then, answer the questions.

Who Discovered America?

In the United States, October 12 is Columbus Day, commemorating the day that Christopher Columbus discovered America. However, many historians now believe that another European discovered North America nearly 500 years before Columbus.

Leif Erikson was the son of Erik the Red, a Norwegian adventurer who moved to Iceland. When he was **exiled** from Iceland, Erik the Red bought a boat to search for new land. He found a huge, ice-covered island that he named Greenland to encourage settlers to come.

Leif Erikson grew up listening to stories about a land that lay to the west of Greenland. In about 1000 AD, Erikson and a small crew sailed in search of this new land. When he and his men reached North America, they found fertile soil, rivers teeming with fish, and thick forests. Erikson was so delighted that he named the land Vinland, which may mean *meadow land* or *pasture land*.

In 1964, the U.S. Congress authorized President Lyndon B. Johnson to proclaim October 9 as Leif Erikson Day. Each year, the current president issues the same proclamation.

23. Which of these statements is true?
    A. Leif Erikson Day is commemorated in the same month as Columbus Day.
    B. The land called Vinland was really the coast of South America.
    C. Erik the Red discovered Vinland.

24. According to the passage, which happened last?
    A. Columbus reached America.
    B. Erik the Red discovered Greenland.
    C. Leif Erikson discovered Vinland.

25. Which of the following best defines the word *exiled*?
    A. banished from one's country
    B. exhausted
    C. given a position of honor in one's own country

FITNESS FLASH: Do 10 shoulder shrugs.

* See page ii.

Change each fraction to a decimal. Then, round each decimal to the nearest hundredth. Finally, write each decimal as a percentage.

1. $\frac{8}{21}$

2. 10.8

3. 12.392

4. 523.32

5. 2.3839

6. $\frac{12}{19}$

7. $\frac{5}{46}$

8. $\frac{11}{23}$

9. $\frac{4}{13}$

10. 2.32

11. 17.45

12. 5.293

An appositive is a noun, a pronoun, or a noun phrase that usually follows another noun or pronoun and describes it. Combine each pair of sentences so that the new sentence has an appositive.

13. Anna got the lead role in the play. Anna is a great actress. _____

_____

14. The United Nations is based in New York City. The United Nations is an influential international organization. _____

_____

15. Bridget and Connor work at the Field Museum in Chicago, Illinois. Bridget and Connor are both geologists. _____

_____

DAY 10

A simile compares two unlike things using the word *like* or *as*. A metaphor also compares unlike things but does not use *like* or *as.* Read each sentence and write **S** for simile or **M** for metaphor. Then, circle the two things being compared.

16. _____ Now in his mid-50s, Roger is as bald as an eagle.

17. _____ My cherished uncle is a treasure to our family.

18. _____ Flying papers and ringing phones created a blizzard of activity in the newsroom.

19. _____ Jumping and pulling at his crimson nose, the clown acted as silly as a goose.

20. _____ Perry runs as fast as a cheetah.

21. _____ Dragging the axle to the aircraft, he certainly proved he's as strong as an ox.

22. _____ With a two-week beach vacation ahead of me, I feel that my life is a dream.

Showing Compassion

Compassion is the act of understanding and being kind to other living beings. There are many ways to show compassion. Treating animals humanely, being empathetic to the misfortune of others, forgiving others, and showing kindness and respect to everyone are just a few ways to show compassion.

Brainstorm a list of ways that you can demonstrate compassion in your community. Consider organizations that need volunteers, make a list of items you no longer need that can be donated, or think of your own project to benefit others living in or near your community. Discuss your list with a parent or family member. Then, put one of your ideas into action this summer.

CHARACTER CHECK: Watch for people who are demonstrating kindness. At the end of the day, share your observations with a family member.

Solve each problem. Round to the nearest hundredth.

1. 20% of 15 = _____

2. _____ % of 70 = 20

3. 65% of _____ = 80

4. 30% of 60 = _____

5. _____ % of 48 = 8

6. 20% of _____ = 75

7. 15% of 75 = _____

8. _____ % of 65 = 33

9. 45% of _____ = 150

10. 37% of 65 = _____

11. _____ % of 9 = 4

12. 22% of _____ = 34

13. 44% of 40 = _____

14. 12% of _____ = 76

15. 50% of _____ = 52

A personal pronoun takes the place of a person or thing. An indefinite pronoun refers generally to a person or a thing. A demonstrative pronoun refers to a specific person or thing. Underline the pronoun in each sentence and identify it. Write *P* for personal, *I* for indefinite, or *D* for demonstrative.

16. _____ Chelsea knows everyone in the room.

17. _____ You are a good photographer.

18. _____ He is running in the race on Saturday.

19. _____ Daniel's father helped them find the keys.

20. _____ It broke yesterday.

21. _____ Lincoln will play tennis with you.

22. _____ Neither was prepared for the pop quiz.

23. _____ They filled the stadium to listen to the candidate speak.

24. _____ These are the items for the canned food drive.

25. _____ I won't go unless Kate goes.

26. _____ That is the easiest way to solve the problem.

27. _____ Many liked the pizza with homemade crust and extra cheese.

28. _____ This is the jacket that Tasha wants.

29. _____ Does anybody know what time it is?

DAY 11

Read each description and write the corresponding source from the word bank.

newspaper or magazine	atlas	encyclopedia
almanac	nonfiction books	Internet

30. contains Web sites about nearly any subject _____

31. contains maps, facts, and figures about various geographical features

    and locations _____

32. contains historical and/or statistical information _____

33. contains up-to-date information about current topics, often organized

    by issue _____

34. organizes facts and information, often alphabetically _____

35. autobiographies, biographies, and other factual information _____

Write the letter of the word from the word bank that matches each description.

A. canyon	B. dune	C. isthmus	D. plateau	E. savanna
F. delta	G. tributary	H. oasis	I. reef	J. strait

36. _____ a sandy hill formed by the wind

37. _____ triangular-shaped land formed by silt deposits at the mouth of a river

38. _____ a fertile area in a desert with a steady water supply

39. _____ a narrow body of water that connects two larger bodies of water

40. _____ a narrow, deep valley with steep sides

41. _____ a large, high, flat area that rises above the surrounding land

42. _____ flat, open grassland with scattered trees and shrubs

43. _____ a smaller river or stream that flows into a larger one

44. _____ a narrow strip of land connecting two larger landmasses

45. _____ sand, rock, or coral at or near the surface of the water

FACTOID: The Nile River is 4,132 miles (6,650 km) long.

Solve each problem.

1. The regular price of a pair of pants is $38.00. The pants are discounted 35%. How much do the pants cost after the discount is applied? _____

2. A bookstore is having a sale. The book Bart wants was originally priced at $14.99. The book is now $10.04. By what percentage was the price reduced? _____

3. Lisa dined at a restaurant and gave the waiter a 15% tip. If the price of her meal was $10.25, how much did Lisa tip the waiter? _____

4. Emily bought a new car for $22,000. She paid 93% of the list price. How much was the list price? _____

A relative pronoun connects a group of words to a noun or a pronoun. An interrogative pronoun introduces a question. Read each sentence. Write _R_ if the underlined pronoun is relative. Write _I_ if the underlined pronoun is interrogative.

5. _____ I will bring <u>whatever</u> you need.

6. _____ <u>What</u> time is your appointment?

7. _____ <u>Which</u> poster won the contest?

8. _____ The essay, <u>which</u> was written by Alyssa, won first place.

9. _____ Choose <u>whichever</u> restaurant you want.

10. _____ <u>What</u> is the title of that song?

11. _____ I don't know <u>what</u> she said.

12. _____ <u>Who</u> brought the chips and juice to the party?

13. _____ I will always remember the nurse <u>who</u> helped me.

14. _____ The child, <u>whom</u> I saw at the parade, was eight years old.

DAY 12

Point of view is the perspective from which a story is told. If a writer tells a story from the first-person point of view, the writer uses *I*. If a writer tells a story from the third-person point of view, the writer uses *he*, *she*, or *they*. Read each sentence. Decide from whose point of view the sentence is being told. Write *F* for first person or *T* for third person.

15. _____ I played a tune on my new harmonica.

16. _____ When the clock struck eight, they walked into town to hear the concert in the square.

17. _____ Sulking, she used her umbrella to shield herself from the rain.

18. _____ I imagined myself as a great singer, performing on stage for a large audience.

19. _____ On a whim, he planted the red geranium in the clay flowerpot.

20. _____ Reading the inscription on the plaque, I was amazed by the building's fascinating history.

21. _____ I speculated that my sister was allergic to the new laundry detergent because of the rash on her arms.

Describe what a typical day would be like from your hand's point of view. How would the world seem different from your hand's perspective?

_____

_____

_____

_____

_____

_____

_____

_____

FITNESS FLASH: Practice a V-sit. Stretch five times.

* See page ii.

Use the order of operations to solve each problem.

1. $2 \times 3[7 + (6 \div 2)] = $ _____

2. $3[-3(2 - 8) - 6] = $ _____

3. $3 \times 3[2 - (9 \div 3)] = $ _____

4. $2[-5(4 - 12) - 3] = $ _____

5. $[(3 \times 3) - (30 \div 6)] + (-27) - 13 = $ _____

6. $2 \div [(4 \div 2) + (32 \div 8)] = $ _____

The case of a pronoun depends upon its use in a sentence. A personal pronoun in the possessive case shows ownership. Write a possessive pronoun to complete each sentence.

7. The watch is _____ .

8. _____ friend is a student here.

9. I thought that book was _____ .

10. We gave the winner _____ approval.

11. _____ card came in the mail yesterday.

12. Are these sunglasses _____ ?

13. This is _____ favorite restaurant.

14. The door was locked, and I did not have _____ key.

15. This is _____ room.

16. The best-disciplined dog in the show is _____ .

17. She was ready to take _____ turn.

18. We plan to take _____ vacation in July.

19. Is this game yours or _____ ?

20. Would you like to hear _____ opinion?

DAY 13

Read the playbill. Then, answer the questions.

Belle of the Ball: A Comedy in Two Acts

by Elizabeth Weaver

Cast: (in order of appearance)

Elizabeth Brown.. Lucy Scott

Belle Brown .... Meg Mitchell

Dressmaker...Susan Moore

Mr. Brown ....Grant Jordan

Mrs. Brown..Jennifer Mills

Ernest Enderby ....Michael Thompson

Clover, the family cat ....Clover

Partygoers: Ben Adams, Ann Davis, Chandra King, Andy Miller, Susan Moore

ACT I

Time: mid-afternoon

Setting: 1920s, the Brown family home

Elizabeth and Belle are in their bedroom preparing for their family's annual ball. The dressmaker is adjusting Elizabeth's gown. Belle is putting the finishing touches on her dress. Mr. and Mrs. Brown talk with Ernest Enderby. Clover emerges from her hiding place under the sofa.

ACT II

Time: evening

Setting: the ballroom

Elizabeth and Belle **mingle** with the partygoers. Belle leads the dancing until the ball is unexpectedly disrupted. The guests gather outside. Ernest Enderby makes an announcement.

---

21. Which actor plays more than one role?

    A. Grant Jordan

    B. Lucy Scott

    C. Susan Moore

22. Which of the following best defines the word *mingle*?

    A. dance

    B. take pictures of

    C. socialize

23. What is the setting for Act II? _____

FACTOID: The average temperature on Mars is -81°F (-63°C).

Solve each problem.

1. -233 − (-233) = _____

2. 31 − (-8) = _____

3. -103 − (-575) = _____

4. -16 − (-38) = _____

5. 43 + (-56) − 78 = ____

6. -78 − 65 = _____

7. -19 − 4 = _____

8. -16 + 9 = _____

9. 71 + (-18) = _____

10. 0 − 17 = _____

11. -8 + (-5) = _____

12. 12 + (-7) = _____

13. -13 + 26 = _____

14. -9 − (-24) = _____

15. 0 − (-9) = _____

A pronoun in the nominative case is a subject, a predicate nominative, or an appositive. A pronoun in the objective case is the object of a verb or a preposition. Circle the pronoun in parentheses that correctly completes each sentence. Then, identify its case. Write **N** for nominative or **O** for objective.

16. _____ One February afternoon, (we, us) went sledding.

17. _____ (She, Her) needs to finish her homework.

18. _____ Most of the students voted for (he, him) to be class president.

19. _____ (They, Them) are our best volleyball players.

20. _____ Call (I, me) when you get home.

21. _____ Please take the gift to (she, her).

22. _____ (They, Them) looked at the map.

23. _____ The teacher helped (he, him) with the math problem.

24. _____ The usher escorted (they, them) to their seats.

25. _____ She sat next to Amy and (I, me).

DAY 14

When you describe the similarities between people, things, or events, you compare them. When you describe their differences, you contrast them. Read the passage and think about the comparisons and contrasts. Then, answer the questions.

Amphibians and reptiles are both cold-blooded animals. Both live in many different areas of the world. Reptiles lay hard-shelled eggs, but amphibians lay soft, sticky eggs. When reptiles hatch, they look like tiny adults. However, amphibians change their appearance throughout several life stages before they finally achieve their mature, adult forms.

26. What two things are being compared in this passage? _____

_____

27. How are the two things similar? How are they different? _____

_____

_____

_____

Would you rather have X-ray vision or the ability to fly? What would you do with each ability? What are their advantages and disadvantages? Explain how you made your choice. Use another piece of paper if you need more space.

_____

_____

_____

_____

_____

_____

_____

_____

FITNESS FLASH: Touch your toes 10 times.

* See page ii.

Solve each problem.

1. $(625 \div 5) \times 0.2 =$ _____

2. $83 + (-85) =$ _____

3. $150/(-5) \times (-4) =$ _____

4. $(-34) + (-255) =$ _____

5. $80 - (-22) =$ _____

6. $28 - (-65) =$ _____

7. $-555/(-5) \times (-6) =$ _____

8. $28 - (-26) =$ _____

9. $-3 \times 5 =$ _____

10. $[-19 - (-20) - (-34)] \div (-6) =$ _____

11. $-424/4 =$ _____

12. $[-18 - (-66) - 22] \times 2 =$ _____

13. $19 - 23 =$ _____

14. $-61 - (-21) =$ _____

15. $(-72/9) + (-64/8) + (44/[-11]) =$ _____

16. $(16 - 21 + 34) \div (-8) =$ _____

Read the paragraph. Replace each underlined noun by writing a pronoun above it. Then, read the new paragraph.

Stepping off the plane, Mrs. Jackson arrived in Costa Rica at noon. As soon as <u>Mrs. Jackson</u> got to her hotel, <u>Mrs. Jackson</u> enjoyed a light lunch at the restaurant. After lunch, Mr. Jackson, who had taken a different flight, joined <u>Mrs. Jackson</u>. "Let's go to the beach," <u>Mr. Jackson</u> said. <u>Mr. and Mrs. Jackson</u> changed into swimsuits, and off <u>Mr. and Mrs. Jackson</u> went. That evening, <u>Mr. and Mrs. Jackson</u> called <u>Mr. and Mrs. Jackson's</u> son, Max. "<u>Mr. and Mrs. Jackson</u> are having a great time," <u>Mr. and Mrs. Jackson</u> told <u>Max</u>.

DAY 15

Write the correct word from the word bank to complete each sentence.

| drama | fable | fantasy | folklore | horror | legend |

17. A _____ is usually written for theatrical performance.

18. A _____ demonstrates a useful truth and often includes talking animals.

19. A _____ invites readers to suspend reality.

20. _____ is usually passed from generation to generation by word of mouth and includes the stories of a people or culture.

21. _____ stories evoke an ominous feeling or dread in both the characters and the reader.

22. A _____ often features a national hero and may be based on real events.

Tree of Balance

Balance and flexibility are important in many sports, from tennis and skiing to football and horseback riding. Try this yoga tree pose, and you will be on your way to having greater balance and flexibility, as well as strength and endurance!

Stand straight with your feet hip-width apart. Raise your arms to the sides at shoulder height. Shift all of your weight to your left leg. Lift your right foot and rotate your knee to the side. Then, touch your right foot to your lower left leg or inner thigh without resting it on your knee. Now, raise your arms straight above your head. Hold this pose for 10 seconds. Slowly bring down your arms and foot. Try the other leg. Think of the foot on the ground as the roots of a tree; press it firmly into the ground. Your arms are the branches. Reach them toward the sky. For better balance, focus your eyes on a fixed point in front of you.

CHARACTER CHECK: Why is honesty important? Write a 30-second commercial promoting honesty. Share it with a family member.

Evaluate each expression given the value of its variable.

1. $y + 2$; $y = 4$

2. $6a/3$; $a = 3$

3. $10d/4 - 8$; $d = 6$

4. $x - 7$; $x = 12$

5. $2c - 4$; $c = 5$

6. $12 - 5z$; $z = 2$

Identify the type of verb or verbs in each sentence. Write *A* for action verb or *L* for linking verb.

7. _____ Todd <u>held</u> the lead after the third day of competition.

8. _____ Lindsey softly <u>blew</u> out the candle when the dinner party <u>was</u> over.

9. _____ The Sonoran Desert seldom <u>gets</u> any snow accumulation.

10. _____ Rockie <u>scratched</u> at the door until someone <u>let</u> him in.

11. _____ There <u>is</u> no justification for their actions.

12. _____ Annie <u>ran</u> out of the apple orchard when a bee <u>buzzed</u> by her head.

13. _____ Joanna <u>cheered</u> as her sister <u>competed</u> in the 100-yard dash.

14. _____ Rachel <u>is</u> the most creative member of the local theater group.

15. _____ Connie and I will <u>be</u> friends forever.

16. _____ I <u>admire</u> people who <u>adopt</u> greyhounds from the Humane Society.

DAY 16

Read the passage. Then, answer the questions.

Types of Rocks

Rocks are classified as igneous, sedimentary, or metamorphic, depending on how they were formed. Igneous rocks form when volcanoes erupt and release a molten rock material called magma. After the magma cools, it forms solid igneous rock. One type of igneous rock is granite, a very hard material often used in construction. Sedimentary rocks form when water deposits sediment, or small pieces of rocks and sand. Over time, sediment compresses into layers. These layers form sedimentary rock, such as limestone. Sedimentary rock often contains fossils and shells. Metamorphic rocks are the least common rock variety. Metamorphic rocks, such as marble, begin as igneous or sedimentary rocks that are squeezed tightly within Earth's crust over a long period of time.

17. What is the main idea of this passage?

    A. Hard rocks can be useful for building sturdy structures.

    B. There are three types of rock that are formed in different ways.

    C. Not all rocks look the same.

18. What are the three types of rocks? _____

    _____

19. How do igneous rocks form? _____

    _____

    _____

20. How do sedimentary rocks form? _____

    _____

    _____

21. How do metamorphic rocks form? _____

    _____

    _____

FACTOID: The muscles that move the eyes contract an average of 100,000 times each day.

Write each expression in exponent form.

1. $3 \cdot 3 \cdot 3 \cdot 3 \cdot 3 \cdot 3$

2. $a \cdot a \cdot b \cdot b \cdot b$

3. $9 \cdot 9$

4. $x \cdot x \cdot x \cdot y$

5. $10 \cdot 10 \cdot 10 \cdot 10 \cdot 10$

6. $4 \cdot 4 \cdot 4 \cdot 4 \cdot 4 \cdot 5 \cdot 5 \cdot 5 \cdot 5$

Simplify each expression.

7. $\dfrac{173,455}{346,910}$

8. $10d + 8 + 4d - 3$

9. $6a - 11a$

An auxiliary verb, or helping verb, combines with the main verb to form the tense. Read each sentence. Underline the main verb once. Then, underline the auxiliary verb twice. Some sentences may have more than one main verb and auxiliary verb.

10. The Saint Bernard has attained a high degree of popularity both as a loyal pet and as a show dog.

11. For many centuries, these hardy animals were used as rescue dogs in the Swiss Alps.

12. They had earned their keep by helping monks find people who were lost in snowstorms.

13. Sometimes, the dogs would work in packs, leading travelers to safety.

14. Saint Bernards are known as excellent guard, herding, and companion dogs.

15. The earliest-known depictions of the breed were painted in 1695.

16. Over the years, Saint Bernards have been known by many names.

17. Some people have called them hospice dogs, Alpine mastiffs, or mountain dogs.

18. The Saint Bernard Club of America was founded in 1888.

19. An adult Saint Bernard can weigh more than 150 pounds.

DAY 17

Write a word from the word bank to complete each sentence.

mystery	poetry	essay	biography	myth

20. A _____ often involves the solution of a crime.

21. A _____ often attempts to explain some natural phenomena and involves the actions of the gods.

22. Verse or rhythmic writing that creates an emotional response is called _____ .

23. A _____ is a factual account of a real person's life.

24. An _____ is a short composition that reflects the author's point of view.

Write the word from the word bank that matches each description.

capital resources	supply	scarcity
demand	inflation	services
goods	natural resources	

25. materials produced for sale _____

26. jobs that people perform for payment _____

27. the amount of goods or services purchased at a given price _____

28. things in nature that have a commercial use or value _____

29. an increase in the average cost of goods and services _____

30. machinery or equipment that produces other goods _____

31. the amount of a product available for sale _____

32. not enough goods and services available to meet demand _____

FITNESS FLASH: Do arm circles for 30 seconds.

* See page ii.

Simplify each problem.

1. $|-12|$

2. $-|10|$

3. $|0|$

4. $|-13| + |-12|$

5. $|-14| - |5|$

6. $-|-15|$

Identify the type of verb that is underlined in each sentence. Write _L_ for linking verb, _AUX_ for auxiliary verb, or _ACT_ for action verb.

7. _____ Matthew <u>is</u> a friend of Chelsea.

8. _____ That puppy <u>is</u> chasing her tail.

9. _____ The farmer <u>turned</u> the soil with a plow.

10. _____ She <u>grew</u> quiet during the conversation.

11. _____ David <u>grew</u> peppers and tomatoes in his garden.

12. _____ He <u>was</u> a magician in the school play.

13. _____ Elizabeth <u>felt</u> the warm sunshine on her face.

14. _____ Gina <u>felt</u> sorry after she dropped the dish.

15. _____ The porch swing <u>is</u> a good spot in which to read.

16. _____ The butterfly <u>was</u> circling the flower.

17. _____ Steve <u>grew</u> a variety of orchid species.

18. _____ Janet <u>has</u> written a fantastic story.

19. _____ The chemist <u>created</u> a new compound.

20. _____ Italian immigrants <u>were</u> registered at Ellis Island.

DAY 18

Write the letter of the word from the word bank that matches each description.

A. conflict	B. foreshadowing	C. irony	D. dialogue
E. imagery	F. point of view	G. hyperbole	H. personification
I. setting	J. allusion		

21. _____ the struggle within a story

22. _____ a reference to a person, place, or event

23. _____ spoken conversation between characters

24. _____ exaggeration for effect

25. _____ hints or clues about what might happen later

26. _____ giving human qualities to animals or objects

27. _____ the perspective from which a story is told

28. _____ the time and place in which a story occurs

29. _____ using words that mean the opposite of what one intends

30. _____ descriptive language that forms vivid mental pictures

Use the words in the word bank to label the paramecium, an animal-like protist.

anal pore	oral groove	food vacuole	cytoplasm
micronucleus	cilia	macronucleus	cell membrane

31. _____

32. _____

33. _____

34. _____

35. _____

36. _____

37. _____

38. _____

FACTOID: One-third of the people on Earth live in China and India.

Write whether each product or quotient is positive or negative.

1. 12.5×5.8 _____

2. $\dfrac{4}{9} \div \left(-\dfrac{3}{10}\right)$ _____

3. $-3\dfrac{1}{7} \div 10\dfrac{4}{5}$ _____

4. $-3\dfrac{1}{5} \times \left(-7\dfrac{3}{8}\right)$ _____

5. $-0.74 \div (-0.17)$ _____

6. $\dfrac{3}{14} \times -\left(\dfrac{2}{7}\right)$ _____

Find each product or quotient.

7. $1.8 \times (-4.5) =$ _____

8. $-9\dfrac{1}{2} \times 3\dfrac{1}{5} =$ _____

9. $-\dfrac{5}{6} \div \left(-\dfrac{7}{8}\right) =$ _____

10. $-\dfrac{4}{5} \times \left(-\dfrac{9}{10}\right) =$ _____

11. $1.782 \times (-2) =$ _____

12. $-4\dfrac{2}{7} \div \left(-3\dfrac{3}{14}\right) =$ _____

Verb tense shows when an action takes place. Write the past tense and past participle of each present-tense verb. Then, use a dictionary to check your work.

Present	Past	Past Participle
13. forget		
14. teach		
15. sink		
16. break		
17. freeze		
18. throw		
19. choose		
20. hear		
21. wake		
22. eat		
23. ride		

DAY 19

Read the passage. Then, answer the questions.

The Blarney Stone

Each year, thousands of tourists visit Blarney Castle in Blarney, Ireland. They come to see, and sometimes kiss, the Blarney Stone, located high in the castle's battlements. The three-story castle was built in 1446 by the King of Munster. The stone that exists today is thought to be half of the original Stone of Scone, which belonged to Scotland. Scottish kings were crowned over the stone because of its alleged magical powers.

How the Blarney Stone earned these alleged powers is unclear. One legend says that an old woman cast a spell on the stone to reward a king for saving her from drowning. Kissing the stone gave the king blarney, which is the ability to speak convincingly.

The term *blarney* may have originated from the many unfulfilled promises of Cormac McCarthy, King of Munster, who promised to give his castle to the Queen of England. But he delayed doing so with soft words, which Queen Elizabeth I described as "blarney talk." Other legends say that the definition came from another king who once lived in the castle. He had the ability to remain in the middle of an argument without taking sides.

Tourists who want to kiss the Blarney Stone do so with great difficulty. They have to lie on their backs and bend backward and down, holding iron bars for support.

24. What is the setting for this passage?
    A. Scotland   B. London   C. Ireland   D. Wales

25. Which of the following best defines the word *blarney*?
    A. understandable conversation   B. confusing speech
    C. skillful flattery or deception   D. nonstop chattering

26. Which of these statements is false?
    A. The present structure of Blarney Castle was built in 1446.
    B. Legends claim that the Blarney Stone gives the gift of convincing speech.
    C. The Blarney Stone is located on the ground floor of Blarney Castle.
    D. Kissing the Blarney Stone is not an easy task.

FITNESS FLASH: Do 10 shoulder shrugs.

* See page ii.

Write the like terms in each problem.

1. $7c + 12c - 2$

2. $12rt - 10r + 18t$

3. $5t + 7t - 1$

4. $19y - 10$

5. $5r - 10r + 8rs$

6. $q + 9 + 2q + 5q$

Simplify the following problems. If the problem is already in its simplest form, write *already simplified.*

7. $8m - 3m$

8. $2 + 10k$

9. $5a + 6a - 9a$

10. $8y + 12y + 3y$

11. $8q + 10q + 14$

12. $t + 8m + 4t - 4m$

Circle the verb or verb phrase in each sentence and identify its tense. Write *PRE* for present tense, *PAST* for past tense, or *FUT* for future tense.

13. _____ I enjoyed seeing the sights in Seattle, Washington.

14. _____ I did not hear you because of the noise in here!

15. _____ Mr. Antonio will teach English at Gibson Middle School this fall.

16. _____ Tracy's dog ate Ms. Chang's new plant.

17. _____ Chase gave his paper to his professor yesterday afternoon.

18. _____ Every autumn, monarch butterflies migrate to Mexico or the California coast.

19. _____ Alyson enjoys the school's spaghetti lunches.

20. _____ The wildfire quickly burned out of control because of the high winds and dry conditions.

21. _____ Mia glanced at the clock every few minutes.

22. _____ Ms. Perez will announce the winner of the essay contest today.

DAY 20

A nonfiction report should be free of bias or personal opinion. Elements of bias may include loaded words, generalizations, and stereotypes. Read the following essay about selecting a pet and underline the elements of bias.

Best Pet

When selecting a family pet, consider getting a turtle. A turtle is the perfect pet for everyone. A turtle needs only a little bit of food each day and, with the proper care, can be a fantastic addition to every home. If you handle a turtle, though, be sure to wash your hands thoroughly afterward. Turtles may carry bacteria called salmonella, which is dangerous to humans.

Granted, all turtles are lazy, as they sit on their rocks in the sun and do not do much else. But, you can sit in a chair and watch them in your free time. Unlike dogs or cats, which are cute and frisky, turtles are sluggish, but still fascinating.

You will need to provide proper food and housing for your turtle. Give it a large tank so that it has plenty of room to roam. Proper lighting is important as well, so you will have to purchase a special ultraviolet lightbulb. Finally, do not forget to name your new pet.

Think of an advertisement you have recently seen or heard. Describe how the advertisement encouraged consumers to buy a company's product. How did the company convey that its product is the best? Should consumers trust all of the information the advertisement provided? Where might you gather more information about the product to make an informed purchase? Use another piece of paper if you need more space.

_____

_____

_____

_____

_____

_____

_____

CHARACTER CHECK: What is compassion? Make a list of five ways that you can show compassion to your friends, family, animals, and the environment.

Resting and Active Pulse Rates

How does exercise affect your heart rate?

Each time the ventricles of your heart contract, blood is forced into your arteries. Each beat of your heart makes your arteries stretch, which causes the pulsing sensation that you feel. As blood is pushed out of your heart with great force, it moves quickly so that it can reach the parts of your body farthest from your heart.

In this activity, you will find your pulse rate and calculate the number of times that your heart beats per minute. Then, you will determine how exercise affects your heart rate.

Materials:
- paper
- chair
- pencil
- stopwatch

Procedure:

1. Sit in a chair and relax for 1 minute. Use your index and middle fingers to locate your pulse on your wrist or neck.

2. Count the number of beats that you feel in 15 seconds. Multiply this number by 4. This is your resting pulse rate for 1 minute. Record this number in the Resting Pulse Rate column.

3. Jog in place for 1 minute. Then, stop jogging and use your index and middle fingers to locate your pulse on your wrist or neck. Calculate your pulse rate as you did in step 2. Record this number in the Active Pulse Rate column.

4. Repeat steps 1 through 3 two additional times. Then, calculate your average resting and active pulse rates by adding the three trials in each column and dividing by 3.

Trial	Resting Pulse Rate	Active Pulse Rate
1		
2		
3		
Average		

5. Ask some friends to find their resting and active pulse rates too. Write your average resting and active pulse rates in the correct columns. Then, calculate the average pulse rates for your friends. Do boys and girls have the same or different average pulse rates? How can you explain this?

* See page ii.

BONUS

Bird Adaptations

How do birds adapt to their environments?

Birds develop different physical features that help them survive. The size and shape of a bird's beak is specific to what it eats. A short, wide beak is usually better for breaking open nuts and seeds. A long, thin beak is better suited to digging for insects and worms. Some birds have longer legs for standing in deep water and catching fish and other water creatures. Other adaptations include size, wingspan, foot type, and feather shape.

In this activity, you will create a model of a bird that is physically adapted to live in a specific habitat.

Materials:
- different colors of clay
- cotton swabs
- buttons
- scissors
- feathers
- drinking straws
- twigs
- glue or glue stick
- construction paper
- chenille stems
- small pebbles

Procedure:
1. Choose one of these habitats.
    A. dry, sandy desert with very little water or plant life
    B. cold, mountainous area; very high elevation
    C. Antarctic region where snow and ice cover the ground year-round
    D. tropical rain forest; full of colorful plant life

2. Use the materials to create a model of a bird that is physically adapted to survive in your chosen habitat.

3. Describe the bird's physical adaptations. _____

_____

_____

4. How might this bird species adapt if humans or nature changed its habitat?

_____

_____

_____

Using Latitude and Longitude

Lines of latitude are imaginary lines on a globe or a map used to measure distances north and south of the equator (0°). They are called *parallels* because they are parallel to the equator. Latitude is written as degrees north or south of the equator. Lines of longitude are imaginary lines on a globe or a map used to measure distances east and west of the prime meridian (0°). Lines of longitude are also known as *meridians,* and they run from the north pole to the south pole. Longitude is written as degrees east or west of the prime meridian.

Use an atlas to find the major city located near each coordinate. Each coordinate is rounded to the nearest degree. Then, write the name of the city on the line.

	City	Latitude	Longitude
1.		22°N	114°E
2.		52°N	1°W
3.		34°N	84°W
4.		56°N	3°W
5.		29°N	77°E
6.		26°S	28°E
7.		41°N	2°E
8.		51°N	114°W
9.		38°N	122°W
10.		24°S	47°W

Use an atlas to plot each city. Then, record the latitude and the longitude on the chart, rounding to the nearest degree.

	City	Latitude	Longitude		City	Latitude	Longitude
11.	Paris			12.	Vancouver		
13.	Beijing			14.	Athens		
15.	Lima			16.	Boston		
17.	Honolulu			18.	Mexico City		
19.	Venice			20.	Moscow		

BONUS

Forms of Government

Many different types of governments exist in the world. Some examples are listed below. Choose three types of governments from the list. Then, with an adult's permission, go online or visit a library to research the three types. Write a brief description of each government.

communism

constitutional democracy

constitutional monarchy

democracy

democratic republic

dictatorship

emirate

federal (federation)

federal republic

Islamic republic

monarchy

oligarchy

parliamentary democracy

parliamentary monarchy

republic

socialism

theocracy

1. _____

_____

_____

_____

_____

2. _____

_____

_____

_____

_____

3. _____

_____

_____

_____

_____

The Panama Canal

Read the passage. Then, create a timeline showing how the Panama Canal came to be.

The Panama Canal crosses the Isthmus of Panama and connects the Atlantic and Pacific Oceans. Early travelers had no choice but to sail around South America to get from one ocean to the other. The idea of building a canal across Panama originated during the early 16th century, but the necessary technology had not yet been developed. In 1880, a French company bought the rights to build the canal and began to dig. However, the land was difficult to clear, and many workers suffered from malaria or yellow fever. Work on the canal came to a halt in 1889. Then, in 1903, the United States bought the rights to build and operate the canal. The project was completed on August 5, 1914.

Because of the difficult land and the great distance that the canal covers, some consider it the greatest modern-age engineering creation. The canal stretches for 50 miles (82 km) from deep water in the Atlantic Ocean to deep water in the Pacific Ocean. Its width varies between 500 to 1,000 feet (150 to 300 m), and its depth is at least 41 feet (12.5 m). The canal uses sets of locks that raise and lower passing ships to the proper level for each ocean. It takes a vessel about 15 to 20 hours to cross from one ocean to the other, including waiting time.

In 1977, U.S. President Jimmy Carter signed the Torrijos-Carter Treaty. This treaty, effective December 31, 1999, began the process of handing over control of the canal to Panama. Since that time, the canal has continued to be a great success. However, the development of wider ships has created problems for when they try to pass through the canal. Work to widen and deepen the canal began in 2007.

BONUS

Take It Outside!

Plan a day trip with your family. Bring a pen, a notebook, and a camera. Every hour on the hour, take a picture of where you are. Make a note of the time and location of each picture. After the trip, print the pictures. Make a timeline of the day, using hours as your time measurement. Place the pictures on the timeline at their appropriate hours. Share your timeline with friends and show them the hourly highlights of your family's day trip.

Find an outdoor movie night or community theater presentation in your area. With a family member, select a movie or performance to attend. Bring a pen and a notebook. If you are watching a live performance, read about the play, director, and actors in the printed program. Take notes about your experience during the show or performance. Afterward, read your notes and write a review of the movie or show. Share your review with family members who attended.

Take a walk around your neighborhood. Bring a pen and a notebook with you. Periodically pause and write notes, indicating what you've done, seen, and heard. After the walk, read your notes. Then, write a 50-word summary of your walk. Edit your summary to 30 words. Be sure to keep the key ideas. Can you edit your piece to a 10-word summary?

* See page ii.

Monthly Goals

Think of three goals to set for yourself this month. For example, you may want to read for 30 minutes each day. Write your goals on the lines. Post them somewhere that you will see them every day.

Draw a check mark beside each goal you meet. Feel proud that you have met your goals and continue to set new ones to challenge yourself.

1. _____

2. _____

3. _____

Word List

The following words are used in this section. Use a dictionary to look up each word that you do not know. Then, write three sentences. Use at least one word from the word list in each sentence.

deficit   innovations
extract   mechanism
gullible   metropolitan
implement   pamphlet
indigenous   segregated

1. _____

_____

2. _____

_____

3. _____

_____

Introduction to Strength

This section includes fitness and character development activities that focus on strength. These activities are designed to get you moving and thinking about strengthening your body and your character.

Physical Strength

Like flexibility, strength is important for a healthy body. Many people think that a strong person is someone who can lift an enormous amount of weight. However, strength is more than the ability to pick up heavy barbells. Having strength is important for many everyday activities, such as helping with yardwork or helping a younger sibling get into a car. Muscular strength also helps reduce stress on your joints as your body ages.

Everyday activities and many fun exercises provide opportunities for you to build strength. Carrying bags of groceries, riding a bicycle, and swimming are all excellent ways to strengthen your muscles. Classic exercises, such as push-ups and chin-ups, are also fantastic strength-builders.

Set realistic, achievable goals to improve your strength based on the activities that you enjoy. Evaluate your progress during the summer months and set new strength goals for yourself as you accomplish your previous goals.

Strength of Character

As you build your physical strength, work on your inner strength as well. Having a strong character means standing up for your beliefs, even if others do not agree with your viewpoint. Inner strength can be shown in many ways. For example, you can show inner strength by being honest, standing up for someone who needs your help, and putting your best effort into every task. It is not always easy to show inner strength. Think of a time when you showed inner strength, such as telling the truth when you broke your mother's favorite vase. How did you use your inner strength to handle that situation?

Use the summer months to develop a strong sense of self, both physically and emotionally. Celebrate your successes and look for ways to become even stronger. Reflect upon your accomplishments during the summer, and you will see positive growth on the inside and on the outside.

Combine like terms.

1. $-n + 9n + 3 - 8 - 8n$

2. $4(x + 9y) - 2(2x + 4y)$

3. $3(-4x + 5y) - 3x(2 + 4y)$

4. $4(x + 5y) + (5x + y)$

5. $5 - 4y + x + 9y$

6. $6x + -2y^2 + 4xy^2 + 3x^2 + 5xy^2$

7. $-2x + 3y - 5x - (-8y) + 9y$

8. $-2(c - d) + (c - 3d) - 5(c - d)$

9. $6(a - b) - 5(2a + 4b)$

10. $3x + (-3y) - (4x) + y$

11. $7(x + 5y) + 3(x + 5y) + 5(3x + 8y)$

12. $-3(4x + -2y) - 2(x + 3y) - 2(2x + 6y)$

13. $12x + 6x + 9x - 3y + (-7y) + y$

14. $2b + 3(2b + 8z) - 3(8b + 2a)$

15. $-21x + (-2x)$

16. $3[2(-y^2 + y) - 3] - 3(2x + y)$

The perfect tense of a verb is formed by adding the present, past, or future tense of _have_ to the past participle of a verb. Complete each sentence with the specified perfect tense of the verb.

17. Preston _____ reading before the rest of us started.
     finish (past perfect)

18. Patricia _____more than 300 miles yesterday.
     drive (past perfect)

19. Myra_____ that aria several times in her career.
     sing (past perfect)

20. Volunteers _____ the nursing home every Sunday.
     visit (present perfect)

21. I _____ a new notebook for biology.
     buy (present perfect)

22. John _____ _Treasure Island_ more than once.
     read (present perfect)

23. Beth's mother _____ the costume before the rehearsal.
     finish (future perfect)

DAY 1

Read each word. Write _P_ if the word has a positive connotation and _N_ if the word has a negative connotation.

24. _____ absurd

25. _____ intrepid

26. _____ radiant

27. _____ assertive

28. _____ thrifty

29. _____ sabotage

30. _____ arrogant

31. _____ obsolete

Write the word from the word bank that matches each description.

diffuse reflection	reflection	opaque	lens	focal point
ray	translucent	convex	transparent	concave

32. _____ a material that allows some light to pass through

33. _____ a material that absorbs or reflects light

34. _____ when light rays hit a rough surface and bounce back at different angles

35. _____ a straight line that represents a light wave

36. _____ when light rays hit a smooth surface and bounce back at the same angle

37. _____ curved outward

38. _____ a curved piece of glass used to refract light

39. _____ a material that allows most light to pass through

40. _____ the point where light waves appear to meet after being reflected by a mirror or lens

41. _____ curved inward

FACTOID: Breakfast cereal was invented in 1863 by James Caleb Jackson.

Circle the correct solution to each equation.

1. $14 - x = 6$
   $x = 4$
   $x = 6$
   $x = 8$

2. $a + 35 = 80$
   $a = 35$
   $a = 40$
   $a = 45$

3. $8 = \dfrac{z}{7}$
   $z = 52$
   $z = 56$
   $z = 63$

4. $4x + 1 = 21$
   $x = 3$
   $x = 4$
   $x = 5$

5. $12 = \dfrac{24}{a}$
   $a = 1$
   $a = 2$
   $a = 3$

6. $10 = 2b + 4$
   $b = 2$
   $b = 3$
   $b = 4$

7. $100 = 142 - t$
   $t = 38$
   $t = 40$
   $t = 42$

8. $6 = 12y - 54$
   $y = 3$
   $y = 4$
   $y = 5$

Find the value of each variable.

9. $m + 7 = 10$ $m = $ _____

10. $40/z = 4$ $z = $ _____

11. $48 - t = 0$ $t = $ _____

12. $8x = 72$ $x = $ _____

Circle the complete verb in each sentence. Then, write the progressive or perfect verb tense.

13. _____ Anna Mason is running for seventh-grade student council representative.

14. _____ Matthew was staying after work for a good reason.

15. _____ My uncle had told his story many times before.

16. _____ The director of marketing will be approving this ad.

17. _____ Larry and Lee have played golf together for years.

18. _____ The trees in our backyard were swaying back and forth during the recent storm.

19. _____ The reporter will be interviewing the eyewitness.

Read the passage. Then, answer the questions.

The Silk Road

The Silk Road was not really a road, nor was it made of silk. The Silk Road refers to a network of trade routes leading from Asia to the West. Many people, including Italian adventurer Marco Polo, traveled along these routes. They often traded goods, such as silk and spices from China, and gold and silver from Italy. However, few people traveled the entire distance of the Silk Road because it was several thousand miles long and very dangerous. The routes covered challenging terrain, such as deserts and mountains, and there was always the danger of meeting bandits. People traded with each other along the way and took goods with them to others farther along the route. In addition to goods, people also traded ideas and inventions along the Silk Road. Travelers even brought such technological innovations as the magnetic compass from Asia to the West.

20. What is the main idea of this passage?
    A. Many people traded goods and ideas along the Silk Road.
    B. The Silk Road was long and dangerous.
    C. Marco Polo traveled along the Silk Road.

21. What was the Silk Road? _____

    _____

22. What did people trade along the Silk Road? _____

    _____

23. Why did few people travel the entire distance of the Silk Road? _____

    _____

24. Write one technological innovation that was brought from Asia to the West.

    _____

FITNESS FLASH: Do five push-ups.

Find the value of each variable.

1. $x - 10 = 23$

2. $t + 3 = 12$

3. $6 + m = -11$

4. $7 + k = 7$

5. $-13 = -6 + s$

6. $7 + r = -7$

7. $7 = 14 + d$

8. $-2 = h + 5$

9. $8 = c + 9$

10. $j + 4 = -15$

11. $p - 5 = -5$

12. $9 = z + 12$

Complete each sentence with the specified perfect tense of the verb.

13. The school board _____that all third-grade students
     (decide–present perfect tense)

     will be immunized against measles.

14. Colin arrived at his appointment more than 30 minutes late and found that

     Dr. Steenburg _____the office.
     (close–past perfect tense)

15. By lunchtime, Dr. Green _____five patients with cavities.
     (see–future perfect tense)

16. Tommy's dad _____ 18 holes of golf before
     (play–future perfect tense)

     Tommy gets out of bed on Saturday morning.

17. The trustees _____ the budget by five percent for the
     (cut–present perfect tense)

     coming year.

DAY 3

Read each sentence. Circle the correct meaning of the underlined word as it is used in the sentence.

18. The farmer made <u>furrows</u> in the earth with the plow.

    A. deep troughs to plant crops in   B. wrinkles in a person's brow

19. My teacher asked me to <u>condense</u> my report to one page.

    A. change from vapor to liquid   B. make shorter or more compact

20. I <u>skimmed</u> the material one more time before the test.

    A. looked at quickly   B. glided across

21. We were asked to <u>refrain</u> from talking during the assembly.

    A. avoid   B. repeated part of a song

22. The city's new development <u>sprawls</u> over many miles.

    A. lies down   B. stretches out

Read the passage. Then, answer the questions.

Community Volunteers

Every community needs volunteers. Some may work with children or the elderly, while others may help clean parks. Some youth organizations require community service hours each month. Groups may hold road races or sell baked goods to support medical research. Others may hold yard sales to raise money for new school equipment. Many communities raise money or provide food, clothing, and shelter for people in need. Volunteering helps people feel that they are giving something back to their communities. A person who receives help today may be able to help others in the future.

23. What is the main idea of this passage?

    A. There are many different ways to volunteer in your community.

    B. Some people like to work in city park.

    C. Many communities raise funds to help others.

24. What are some ways that people can help their communities? _____

    _____

    _____

FACTOID: Earth is 7,926 miles (12,756 km) in diameter.

Use the commutative property to create new equations.

1. $6 + y = 12$

2. $56 = t \cdot 7$

3. $a + 17 = 21$

4. $11 + k = 32$

5. $x + 4 = 12$

6. $3 = r + 8$

7. $h \cdot 15 = 75$

8. $39 = 13 \cdot f$

The simple subject and the verb of a sentence must agree. Underline the subject of each sentence. Then, circle the verb that correctly completes each sentence.

9. The beads (is, are) missing from the bag.

10. The gate (is, are) on the left side of her house.

11. Tucson (lies, lie) to the south of Phoenix, Arizona.

12. The Hawks, the Eagles, and the Cardinals (is, are) all divisional leaders.

13. The tower (is, are) part of the city skyline.

Write a verb that agrees with the subject to complete each sentence.

14. Robert and Melody_____ their homework immediately after school.

15. If the sun has set, the cows_____ in the barn.

16. Tourists _____ every winter to warmer climates.

17. Christie_____more quietly than Olivia.

18. The home team's fans always _____ great sportsmanship.

DAY 4

A root word is a word that has a prefix, a suffix, or both added to it. Read each word. Write the root word and the prefix or the suffix on the correct lines. Some words will have either a prefix or a suffix, and some words may have both a prefix and a suffix.

	Prefix	Root Word	Suffix
19. beautiful	_____	_____	_____
20. kindness	_____	_____	_____
21. friendly	_____	_____	_____
22. cheerful	_____	_____	_____
23. incomplete	_____	_____	_____
24. treeless	_____	_____	_____
25. indefinitely	_____	_____	_____

Plank Practice

Strong muscles and bones are important for fitness and overall health. Strengthen your arms, back, wrists, and abdomen with the yoga plank pose.

While it may seem easy, this yoga pose can be very challenging, so start slowly. Begin by lying on your stomach. Place your hands by your shoulders with your palms flat on the floor. Lift yourself into a push-up position. Align your head and neck with your back and keep your back flat. Your shoulders should be directly above your elbows. Now, tighten your abdomen. If this is too difficult, lower your knees to the floor. Remember to breathe. Hold the pose for 10 seconds. Then, slowly lower yourself to the starting position. Repeat this activity two or three times.

FITNESS FLASH: Do 10 lunges.

* See page ii.

Rewrite each expression using the associative property. Then, evaluate the expression.

1. 8 + (2 + 17)

2. (3 • 25) • 4

3. 75 + (25 + 19)

4. (3 • -4) • 250

5. (21 + 45) + 55

6. -20 • (50 • -29)

7. 68 + (32 + 54)

8. (12 • 5) • 20

9. 5 • (10 • 18)

Underline the subject(s) of each sentence. Then, circle the verb that correctly completes each sentence.

10. Gretchen (goes, go) home every weekend to see her parents.

11. Carlos and Ben (has been, have been) friends since third grade.

12. A statue of Andrew Jackson (stands, stand) in the middle of Jackson Square in New Orleans, Louisiana.

13. Two professional baseball teams (calls, call) New York City their home.

14. Trail Ridge Road (winds, wind) its way through Rocky Mountain National Park.

15. The questions (was, were) difficult for the candidate.

16. The president and vice president (runs, run) as a team during a presidential election.

17. Kiley (brings, bring) her pet lizard to school every year for "Pets on Parade Week."

DAY 5

Read the passage. Then, answer the questions.

Jackie Robinson (1919–1972)

Jackie Robinson's interest in sports began early in his life. He attended college at UCLA and lettered in baseball, basketball, football, and track. When Robinson, an African American, was growing up, sports teams were **segregated**. Black athletes and white athletes could not play together. Only white players were allowed to be on professional sports teams.

Jackie Robinson pioneered racial integration in professional sports. In 1947, he joined the Brooklyn Dodgers, a New York baseball team. Many fans were angry that an African American was on the team. Some wrote threatening letters; others mocked Robinson on the field. Some players did not want him on the team. But, he did not give up; he kept playing. He did so well his first season that he was named Rookie of the Year.

In the 10 years that Jackie Robinson played for the Dodgers, the team won six National League pennants and played in the World Series. Robinson retired in 1956, later raising money for the National Association for the Advancement of Colored People (NAACP) and speaking for the rights of African Americans. He also was elected to the Baseball Hall of Fame. Robinson broke the color barrier in major league baseball, which opened the sports world to other African American players.

18. Choose a good title for this passage.
    - A. Breaking the Color Barrier in Sports
    - B. A Great Baseball Player
    - C. Jackie Robinson's College Years
    - D. Rookie of the Year

19. What does the word *segregated* mean in the story?
    - A. forced to play together
    - B. divided into teams
    - C. kept apart by race
    - D. mixed together

20. Number the following events in the order in which they happened.

    _____ Robinson retires from professional baseball.

    _____ Robinson is elected to the Baseball Hall of Fame.

    _____ Robinson joins the Brooklyn Dodgers.

    _____ Robinson letters in four college sports.

21. Why was Robinson's baseball career important? _____

    _____

CHARACTER CHECK: Make a list of five things you can do at home that demonstrate cooperation. Post the list and invite family members to add to it.

Complete each equation.

1. $a + 3a = 1a + 3a = (1 + \underline{\quad\quad}) a$ 2. $(6t + 5t) = \underline{\quad\quad} (6 + 5)$

Rewrite each expression using the distributive property. Do not simplify.

3. $4(12 + 15)$

4. $3a + 6b$

5. $(10 + 13)t$

6. $x(6 + 8)$

7. $7r + 8r + 2$

8. $2(5x + 8y)$

Use the distributive property to simplify each expression.

9. $7a + a + 15$

10. $k + 5 + 7 + 3k$

11. $2(b + 4) + 8b$

12. $2c + 6c + 9(c + 3)$

When the subject of a sentence performs the action, the verb is in the active voice. When the subject of a sentence is being acted upon, the verb is in the passive voice. Rewrite each sentence in the active voice.

13. I was fascinated by the movie, *The Sound of Music*. _____

_____

14. The young children in the classroom were amazed by the deputy's words.

_____

_____

15. The toy was chased by Meghan's cat, Buffy. _____

_____

16. Lucy was sprayed in the face when she opened the soft drink.

_____

_____

17. A goal was scored by Andy Rahal of the Crosby Middle School soccer team.

_____

_____

DAY 6

Circle the word that correctly completes each analogy.

18. Stiff is to flexible as empty
    is to _____ .
    A. low   B. rigid
    C. full   D. elastic

19. Glass is to transparent as wood
    is to _____ .
    A. clear   B. opaque
    C. pine   D. fragile

20. Waltz is to dance as oak
    is to _____ .
    A. acorn   B. tree
    C. pine   D. tango

21. Laugh is to tickle as shiver
    is to _____ .
    A. cold   B. bored
    C. giggle   D. amused

22. Star is to galaxy as word
    is to _____ .
    A. universe   B. alphabet
    C. planet   D. dictionary

23. Thrifty is to cheap as smart
    is to _____ .
    A. dull   B. foolish
    C. gullible   D. brilliant

24. A chapter is to a book as an act
    is to a _____ .
    A. novel   B. comedy
    C. play   D. sitcom

25. Precise is to exact as lively
    is to _____ .
    A. energetic   B. listless
    C. inaccurate   D. quick

Think of your favorite food. Now, explain to someone who has just moved to this country how your favorite food tastes. Describe the flavors by comparing them to other foods this person might have experienced already. Use another piece of paper if you need more space.

_____

_____

_____

FACTOID: A newborn giant panda weighs 3–5 ounces (85–142 g).

Solve each proportion. Use cross products.

1. $\dfrac{1}{4} = \dfrac{x}{8}$

2. $\dfrac{20}{30} = \dfrac{5}{d}$

3. $\dfrac{18}{24} = \dfrac{12}{l}$

4. $\dfrac{80}{m} = \dfrac{48}{20}$

5. $\dfrac{5}{5} = \dfrac{5n}{5}$

6. $\dfrac{15}{45} = \dfrac{3}{t}$

7. $\dfrac{1.8}{v} = \dfrac{3.6}{2.8}$

8. $\dfrac{8}{z} = \dfrac{5}{2}$

9. $\dfrac{8}{6} = \dfrac{s}{27}$

10. $\dfrac{144}{6} = \dfrac{6c}{6}$

11. $\dfrac{r}{3} = \dfrac{8}{8}$

12. $\dfrac{36}{12} = \dfrac{b}{6}$

13. $\dfrac{0.14}{0.07} = \dfrac{k}{1.5}$

14. $\dfrac{6}{w} = \dfrac{6}{4}$

15. $\dfrac{4}{5} = \dfrac{f}{5}$

16. $\dfrac{16}{48} = \dfrac{h}{50}$

An adjective describes a noun or a pronoun. A descriptive adjective answers the question *what kind*. A limiting adjective answers the questions *which one* or *how many*. Circle the adjectives in each sentence. Write *D* above each descriptive adjective and *L* above each limiting adjective.

17. Four million visitors were attracted this year to beautiful, majestic Yosemite National Park.

18. Mark spent a long time preparing his interesting and detailed speech on human rights.

19. Three lost campers were delighted to see the two park rangers who had been looking for them.

20. I attended a smaller school before coming to this one.

21. Andy is both taller and heavier than Stephen.

22. Annie's bright, cheerful personality can fill a room with joy.

DAY 7

Read each sentence and write *S* for simile and *M* for metaphor. Then, circle the two things that are being compared in each sentence.

23. _____ Detective Oakley is as sly as a fox.

24. _____ With my family and friends joining me for dinner, I felt as happy as a lark.

25. _____ My love for my puppy, Sparky, is as strong as steel.

26. _____ After five swimming lessons, Louise swam through the water as fast as a fish.

27. _____ "Your hand is as cold as ice," said Pat.

28. _____ His grandson is the sunshine of Mr. Frank's life.

29. _____ When it comes to grudges, Ralph is a stubborn mule.

Read the first word pair. Make the next word pair by taking the second word from the previous word pair and combining it with a word from the word bank. Words pairs must combine to form either a compound word or words that are often used together. The goal is to reach the last word pair provided.

ball	dragon	finger	fly	snap
dragon	finger	fly	ring	snap

30. key, ring

31. _____

32. _____

33. _____

34. _____

35. _____

36. ball, game

FITNESS FLASH: Do 10 sit-ups.

* See page ii.

Solve each problem. Round each answer to two decimal places.

1. If 3 square feet of fabric costs $3.75, what would 7 square feet cost?

2. A 12-ounce bottle of soap costs $2.50. How many ounces would be in a bottle that costs $3.75?

3. Four pounds of apples cost $5.00. How much would 10 pounds of apples cost?

4. A 12-ounce can of lemonade costs $1.32. How much would a 16-ounce can of lemonade cost?

5. A 32-pound box of cantaloupes costs $24.40. How much would a 12-pound box cost?

6. If a 10-pound turkey costs $20.42, how much does a 21-pound turkey cost?

An adjective has three degrees of comparison: positive, comparative, and superlative. Write the correct form of each adjective in parentheses to complete each sentence.

7. (sympathetic) Jason is _____ to the thoughts of others.

8. (honest) Joanna is the _____ person I've ever known.

9. (active) Leah is_____than her sister Elena.

10. (monstrous) Mrs. Cravens gave us a _____ assignment for tomorrow.

11. (ominous) The dark clouds provided our cookout with a _____

    setting than we would have chosen.

12. (young) The _____ student in our class is also one of

    the most talented.

13. (famous) Todd's tournament win made him Spokane's _____

    _____ citizen.

DAY 8

Read the passage. Then, answer the questions.

What's in a Coral Reef?

A coral reef is like a complex city that supports a dazzling array of life almost as diverse as that of a rain forest. The architects of these underwater habitats are animals called coral polyps. Usually no bigger than peas, coral polyps look like tiny, colorful flowers.

Coral polyps extract calcium from seawater and convert it to limestone. The limestone forms little cups of rock to support their soft bodies. Each polyp attaches to its neighbor with the skeleton formed by its outer skin, forming coral colonies. As polyps grow, they build new cup skeletons on top of old ones. Limestone formations built by millions of coral polyps are called coral reefs. Structures formed by the polyps may be branches, cups, ripples, discs, fans, or columns. Each kind of coral grows in a specific pattern.

Densely populated coral reefs provide habitats for an amazing **diversity** of marine life, including neon-colored fish, moray eels, soft corals, sponges, tube worms, barracuda, sharks, starfish, manta rays, sea turtles, lobsters, crabs, and shrimp.

Coral fossils indicate that coral reefs have existed for millions of years. The solid appearance of reefs might lead us to think that they are permanent. However, coral reefs are fragile, carefully balanced ecosystems that are easily threatened. A change in the temperature, water quality, or light can kill the coral polyps.

Some destruction of coral reefs may result from these natural causes, but humans cause the greatest damage to reefs. Once a reef is damaged, it may never recover, and the entire coral community may be lost.

14. Why are coral reefs described as complex cities? _____

_____

15. Which of the following best defines the word *diversity*?
    A. a home for marine animals
    B. a variety
    C. a school of brightly colored fish
    D. a specific pattern

16. The diversity of coral reefs is second only to the diversity found in
    A. the Arctic tundra.
    B. the grasslands.
    C. rain forests.
    D. swamps and wetlands.

17. Why do polyps extract calcium from seawater? _____

_____

FACTOID: Australia's Great Barrier Reef can be seen from outer space.

Write a proportion to represent each problem. Solve the proportion.

1. 45 is what percentage of 90? _____

2. What percentage of 100 is 19? _____

3. What is 75% of 60? _____

4. 35% is 7 out of what number? _____

5. 62% of what number is 9.5? _____

6. 60% of what number is 50.4? _____

7. 7 out of 28 is what percentage? _____

8. 90 is 100% of what number? _____

9. How much is 72% of 54? _____

10. What percentage of 132 is 76.56? _____

Identify the part of speech of each underlined word. Write *P* for pronoun or *A* for adjective.

11. _____ This is <u>my</u> best friend.

12. _____ Bruce will buy <u>whichever</u> is left.

13. _____ Emma can buy <u>any</u> book she wants.

14. _____ Was Bob interested in <u>them</u>?

15. _____ <u>This</u> is my favorite flavor of ice cream.

16. _____ Betty ate <u>some</u> of these carrots with dip.

17. _____ <u>Those</u> girls read *Wuthering Heights* this summer.

18. _____ <u>Each</u> one found a seat in the theater.

19. _____ <u>Those</u> weren't on the shelf.

20. _____ Cheryl doesn't want <u>any</u>, but McKenna would like a brownie.

DAY 9

Read each sentence. Use the context clues to determine the definition of each boldfaced word. Then, write the letter of the correct definition on the line.

21. _____ My **initial** impression was that soccer was a difficult game, but I soon changed my mind.

22. _____ The **narrator** of the documentary spoke in a very soft voice.

23. _____ Volunteers distributed **pamphlets** listing ways that people could help the environment.

24. _____ We will **implement** our new plan next week.

25. _____ I have a strong **hunch** that it will snow tomorrow.

26. _____ Mom is good at **motivating** me to try to do well.

27. _____ Last year, we moved from a rural area to a **metropolitan** region.

28. _____ Candace **excels** at math and science.

A. put into action

B. first, or at the beginning

C. area around and including a city

D. someone speaking

E. inspiring

F. small, printed papers

G. feeling or guess

H. does well

Demonstrating Integrity

Integrity means having sound moral principles and being upstanding, honest, and sincere. Select one of the following situations. Draw two four-panel comic strips to show possible consequences of demonstrating and not demonstrating integrity.

• You are at the movies with friends. While in line at the concession stand, you realize that you do not have enough money to buy everything you want. You notice that a person in front of you has unknowingly dropped a five-dollar bill on the floor.

• You are having fun swimming with your best friend and other good friends from school. Your best friend wants to stay longer, and you really want to stay too. However, you promised to help your grandparents with a project later that day. If you stay at the pool with your friends, you will not be able to help your grandparents.

FITNESS FLASH: Do 10 squats.

* See page ii.

Plot and label the following points on the graph.

A (3,-4)

B (6,2)

C (0,-2)

D (1,7)

E (3,-3)

F (2,-6)

G (-3,4)

H (-1,-4)

I (3,0)

J (2,5)

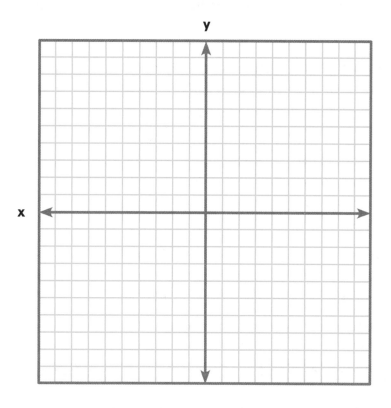

An adverb modifies a verb, an adjective, or another adverb. Circle each adverb and draw an arrow to the word that it modifies. There may be more than one adverb in each sentence.

1. Luis and Miguel are identical twins, but they have vastly different personalities.

2. Michelle, our art director, attracted exceptionally talented artists to our company.

3. Anthony bravely donned his coat, gloves, and scarf before he stepped outside.

4. John and Suzie came to our costume party uniquely dressed as a king and a queen.

5. The students in Mr. Andrew's class showed a really wonderful attitude about the difficult assignment.

6. The table centerpiece is a professionally arranged bouquet.

7. Elizabeth removed her shoes so that she could quietly tiptoe through the house.

8. If I win an award, I will be truly happy.

DAY 10

Read each sentence. Use the context clues to determine the definition of each boldfaced word. Then, write the letter of the correct definition on the line.

9. _____ Ms. Yang **demonstrated** the experiment.

10. _____ My brother and I **typically** spend each summer at our grandmother's house.

11. _____ The sportscaster **predicted** that the visiting team would win the game.

12. _____ My **schedule** includes activities every day after school.

13. _____ The coach asked us to keep our plans **flexible** in case our team made the play-offs.

14. _____ Eating a variety of foods **nourishes** the body.

15. _____ Mom fixed the **mechanism** so that she could move the garage door up and down.

16. _____ The jury had reached a **verdict**.

A. foretold

B. mechanical device

C. showed how to do

D. changeable

E. provides nutrients for

F. usually

G. decision

H. plans

Write the word from the word bank that matches each description.

| lithosphere | outer core | inner core |
| mantle | atmosphere | crust |

17. _____ layer of molten iron and nickel that surrounds the inner core

18. _____ thinnest, outermost layer of Earth; ranges from about 3 miles (5 km) to 62 miles (100 km) thick

19. _____ layer of hot, solid material between the crust and Earth's core

20. _____ rigid layer consisting of the crust and outermost part of the mantle

21. _____ dense sphere of solid iron and nickel at the center of Earth

22. _____ soft layer of the mantle on which pieces of lithosphere slowly float

CHARACTER CHECK: Look up the word *responsible* in a dictionary. How do you demonstrate responsibility?

Write the moves you would make to graph each ordered pair.

1. (3,-2)_____
2. (-1,4)_____
3. (7,6) _____
4. (-4,-5)_____
5. (0,-3)_____
6. (7,0) _____

Write the coordinates of each point.

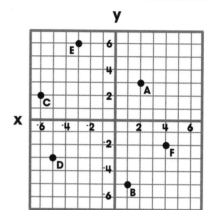

7. A _____
8. B _____
9. C _____
10. D _____
11. E _____
12. F _____

Like adjectives, adverbs have three degrees of comparison: positive, comparative, and superlative. Write the correct form of each adverb in parentheses to complete each sentence.

13. (costly) Raising tropical fish can be _____

   than other hobbies because it doesn't involve paying a lot of vet bills.

14. (beautifully) The sun set _____ over Yellowstone National Park.

15. (badly) I did not give Boz a treat because he behaved _____

   than yesterday.

16. (slowly) The snail moves the _____of the three animals.

17. (thoroughly) Mia usually completes her homework assignments_____

   _____ than her friend Angie.

18. (closely) The broker followed the stock market _____

   than usual because of yesterday's wild day of trading.

DAY 11

Read the passage. Then, answer the questions.

An Egyptian Board Game

Alquerque (pronounced ahl-CARE-kay) is a two-player board game that originated in Egypt. It is similar to checkers.

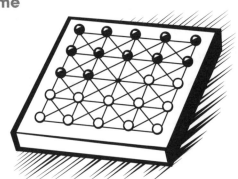

Materials: Game board and 24 game pieces (12 of one color, 12 of another)

Object of the Game: Players capture opponent's pieces by jumping over them.

Game Setup: Players face each other with the board between them and arrange the game pieces according to the illustration.

To Play: A coin toss determines which player moves first. Players can move along the lines of the board horizontally, vertically, diagonally, or backward. A player can move only one space at a time unless he is capturing an opponent's piece. A player captures an opponent's piece if the piece is next to the player's piece and if the space beyond the opponent's piece is vacant. To take a piece, a player jumps over it into the empty space and removes the captured piece from the board. The player's turn continues until he can make no more captures. Players can choose not to move after taking a piece.

To Win: The game ends when a player captures all of the opponent's pieces or when neither player can make a capture. The player with the most captured pieces wins.

19. A piece can move
    A. two spaces at a time
    B. vertically, backward, horizontally, and diagonally
    C. only vertically and diagonally

20. Read each statement. Write *T* if the statement is true. Write *F* if the statement is false.

    _____ Alquerque is a two-player game.

    _____ Alquerque is similar to chess.

    _____ Players must move again after capturing an opponent's piece.

    _____ The game ends when a player moves two pieces to the opposite end.

FACTOID: More than one-fifth of the land on Earth is desert.

Write the letter of each word next to its definition.

1. _____ two angles with a side and vertex in common

   A. area

2. _____ pairs of angles that lie outside the parallel lines on opposite sides of the transversal

   B. congruent angles

3. _____ pairs of angles that lie between the parallel lines on opposite sides of the transversal

   C. alternate interior angles

4. _____ two angles whose measurements equal 180°

   D. volume

5. _____ the amount of space within a three-dimensional figure (measured in cubic units)

   E. supplementary angles

6. _____ the sum of the areas of all of the faces of a three-dimensional figure

   F. complementary angles

7. _____ the distance around a two-dimensional, closed figure

   G. adjacent angles

8. _____ pairs of angles that appear in corresponding positions in the two sets of angles that were formed by the parallel lines cut by the transversal

   H. alternate exterior angles

9. _____ angles with equivalent measurements

   I. perimeter

10. _____ two angles whose measurements equal 90°

   J. surface area

11. _____ the perimeter of a circle

   K. circumference

12. _____ the surface space within a two-dimensional, closed figure (measured in square units)

   L. corresponding angles

Identify the underlined word in each sentence. Write _ADJ_ for adjective and _ADV_ for adverb.

13. _____ April answered the questions as accurately as she <u>possibly</u> could.

14. _____ The center, Rex, is the <u>tallest</u> player on our basketball team.

15. _____ Miss Gray's test today was the most <u>difficult</u> one she has given all year.

16. _____ His cousin is a reporter who appears <u>nightly</u> on a local news show.

17. _____ How <u>quickly</u> does our new employee type on his computer?

18. _____ Tonight <u>probably</u> will be a great night to see the meteor shower.

19. _____ Do you think that the World Wide Web was the <u>most</u> useful technological invention of the 20th century?

DAY 12

Read the passage. Then, answer the questions.

The Science of Sleep

Every living creature needs sleep. You may not realize it, but many important things happen to your body and mind during sleep. While you sleep, your heart, lungs, muscles, nervous system, digestive system, and skeletal system rest and prepare for another day. Your body repairs itself during this time. Getting enough sleep also helps your body fight sickness.

Insufficient sleep results in sleep debt, or an amount of sleep that is owed to your body. Sleep debt affects how you function. People with this deficit may not think that they are sleepy, but they are less able to concentrate or learn new information. They may be irritable, emotional, or have a slower reaction time.

During sleep, your body passes through a five-stage cycle. In the first stage, you are either just beginning to fall asleep or are sleeping lightly. During the second stage, your breathing and heart rate become regular, and your body temperature starts to drop. The third and fourth stages are the deepest, most restful stages of sleep. Throughout these stages, your muscles relax, and your breathing and heart rate become slow and regular. During the fifth and final stage of sleep, your brain gets the critical rest that it needs to function well the next day. During this last stage of sleep, you reach and maintain rapid eye movement (REM), which means that your eyeballs move rapidly under your closed eyelids. REM is also the stage of sleep in which you dream. An entire sleep cycle lasts about 100 minutes and is repeated five or six times every night.

Every individual has his own sleep needs, but researchers have determined that teens need between 8.5 and 9.25 hours of sleep each night to restore full brain function the following day.

20. Write the main idea of the passage. _____

_____

21. Underline three details in the passage that support the main idea.

Use the Internet to research making compost for a garden. Find different methods used to make compost. On another sheet of paper, write a paragraph to explain each method. Use a strong topic sentence and supporting details in each paragraph.

FITNESS FLASH: Do five push-ups.

* See page ii.

Name each point, line, line segment, or ray.

1.
_____

2.
_____

3.
S
_____

4.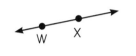
_____

5.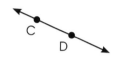
_____

6.
_____

7.
_____

8.
•
M
_____

9.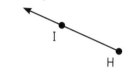
_____

A preposition shows the relationship of a noun or a pronoun to another word in the sentence. A preposition often describes direction, time, place, manner, cause, or amount. Write a preposition or prepositions to complete each sentence.

10. Aaron Machovich has been one _____ the best football players ever to play _____ Roosevelt High School.

11. Students should be sitting _____ their seats before the final bell rings.

12. If you think you can keep up _____ the field, you should enter the marathon.

13. I keep my keys _____ the door so that I do not forget them.

14. If you take the ice _____ the freezer too soon, it will melt.

15. Evelyn Rae was the valedictorian _____ our graduating class.

16. I usually place a cover _____ the grill when I'm finished cooking to prevent dust and dirt from collecting _____ the grill plates.

17. We learned how to use a fire extinguisher_____ case of an emergency.

18. Molly crouched _____ the plate, although she feared being hit _____ a fast pitch.

19. Louis wore his new pair _____ shoes to the dance.

DAY 13

When you summarize a story or article, you use your own words to give only the most important information. Write a two-sentence summary of the passage.

Marsha Finds a Pet

All Marsha ever wanted was a pet of her own. On her 13th birthday, Marsha's mother agreed to let her adopt a puppy. They rode the trolley to the local animal shelter. First, Marsha saw a six-month-old cocker spaniel. The puppy was cute, but it was not quite right for her. Then, Marsha saw a golden-haired collie running in circles and trying to catch his tail. "That's the one!" Marsha exclaimed, laughing excitedly and pointing with great satisfaction. Marsha had found the pet of her dreams.

_____

_____

_____

_____

Wall-Sit Challenge

Wall-sits are a great way to increase lower-body strength. Begin by standing with your back about two feet from a wall. Then, while leaning against the wall, slide down, bending your knees until your thighs are parallel to the ground (at about a 90-degree angle). You should feel like you are sitting in an imaginary chair. Hold that position for 10 seconds, and then stand up. Try again, holding the position for as long as you can. As an additional challenge, try raising one leg at a time for a few seconds while holding the position. Set monthly goals to increase the length of time that you stay in a wall-sit and enjoy the benefit of a strong lower body.

FACTOID: Only one percent of the world's water is drinkable.

* See page ii.

Identify each angle as acute, obtuse, right, or straight.

1. m ∠RST = 180° _____
2. m ∠XYZ = 135° _____
3. m ∠ABC = 45° _____
4. m ∠IJK = 100° _____
5. m ∠TUV = 90° _____
6. m ∠GHI = 80° _____

Identify each angle as acute, obtuse, right, or straight.

7.

_____

8.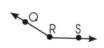

_____

9.

_____

10.

_____

11.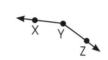

_____

12.

_____

Draw and label each of the following angles.

13. acute angle HIJ
14. obtuse angle DEF
15. right angle GHI

A prepositional phrase includes a preposition, its object, and all of the words that modify the object. In each sentence, underline each prepositional phrase and circle its preposition.

16. Audrey left her wallet by the phone in the Louisville, Kentucky, airport.

17. The mayor's wife enjoyed entertaining people who did business with the city.

18. I cannot possibly complete my report without that information.

19. The bird in the tree is a yellow finch.

20. Jonathan saved enough allowance money to go to the movies.

21. Pete brought his expertise to the booth as a member of the new broadcast team.

22. If you are missing any money, check under the cushions of the sofa.

23. The tunnel followed a path under the two buildings.

24. Marc always orders baked ziti at Italian restaurants.

DAY 14

Read the passage. Then, answer the questions.

National Parks

National parks are areas of land set aside to preserve wildlife and to offer places where visitors can experience and enjoy natural settings. Laws protect these parks so that people cannot use them to profit, hunt animals, or damage plants in any way.

In the 1800s, fewer than 10 national parks existed in Canada and the United States. Yellowstone, the first U.S. national park, was established in 1872. Yellowstone covers parts of three states. It is famous for its geysers, hot springs, and scenery. Canada established its first national park in 1885. Banff National Park in Alberta sits in the Rocky Mountains and is known for its mountains, its glaciers, its array of wildlife, and Lake Louise.

Eventually, the idea of national parks caught on internationally during the late 1800s and early 1900s. National parks now protect the world's highest mountains, largest waterfalls, and other important natural features on nearly every continent.

Many national parks experience problems protecting their natural environments. Native animals can reproduce rapidly and overpopulate the areas. The large volume of park visitors can make controlling misuse difficult. The huge size of some parks also makes protected animals easy targets for **poachers**.

Even with these problems, national parks are wonderful places to visit. National parks can help people appreciate nature and learn more about the world.

25. What is the main idea of this passage?

    A. National parks can be found all over the world.

    B. National parks are places set aside to preserve nature.

    C. Many plants and animals are safe in national parks.

26. What is Banff National Park known for? _____

    _____

27. Name two problems facing national parks. _____

    _____

28. What is Yellowstone National Park famous for? _____

    _____

29. What is a *poacher*?

    A. a fried egg   B. an angry deer   C. an illegal hunter

FITNESS FLASH: Do 10 lunges.

* See page ii.

Name each angle. Then, use a protractor to measure it.

1.
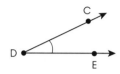

∠ _____ = _____
    angle   degrees

2.

∠ _____ = _____
    angle   degrees

3.
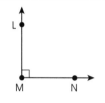

∠ _____ = _____
    angle   degrees

4.
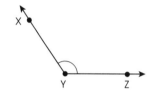

∠ _____ = _____
    angle   degrees

A coordinating conjunction connects similar words, phrases, and clauses. Write a coordinating conjunction to complete each sentence.

5. Roses need excellent drainage, _____ their leaves will turn yellow.

6. Eugene wanted a pet that was exotic_____unusual.

7. It is possible,_____ it is not very likely.

8. We waited in the terminal for hours, _____ our connection never arrived.

9. He was born and raised in Ohio, _____ he now lives in New York.

10. Zoe decides on the itinerary, _____ Joe makes the travel arrangements.

11. Sam has been driving_____making sales calls for weeks.

12. I cannot attend the wedding, _____Janet can.

13. Gerald bought celery _____ onions at the grocery store.

14. Carmen_____ Mimi registered for classes.

DAY 15

Write the letter of the word that matches each definition.

15. _____ a comparison that does not use the words *like* or *as*

    A. alliteration

16. _____ the formal rhythm of a poem, often used with rhyme

    B. metaphor

17. _____ a comparison using the words *like* or *as*

    C. rhyme

18. _____ use of words that start with the same sound

    D. assonance

19. _____ a word or phrase that sounds like what it describes

    E. meter

20. _____ use of words that end with the same sound

    F. rhythm

21. _____ repeated vowel sounds

    G. free verse

22. _____ the beat of a poem

    H. onomatopoeia

23. _____ poetry without a set meter or rhyme scheme

    I. simile

Read the clues that describe each type of rock. Write the correct word from the word bank for each set of clues.

limestone	slate	granite	marble

24. I am an igneous rock.
I am intrusive.
I have large mineral grains.
Because of my strength, I am often used to make headstones.
Which rock am I?_____

25. I am a sedimentary rock.
I am made of calcium carbonate.
I am found where water once stood.
Gas bubbles appear when acid touches me.
Which rock am I?_____

26. I am a metamorphic rock.
I am a foliated rock.
I am formed from shale.
My minerals are so compact that I am watertight.
Which rock am I?_____

27. I am a metamorphic rock.
I am a non-foliated rock.
I am formed from limestone.
Artists often use me to create sculptures.
Which rock am I?_____

CHARACTER CHECK: At the end of the day, think about how you demonstrated loyalty during the day. Why is loyalty an important quality?

Use the figure to the right to answer each question.

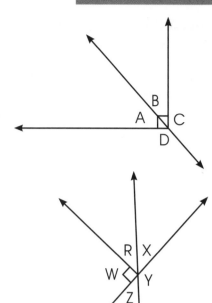

1. m∠A + m∠B = _____ °

   This is called a _____ angle.

2. m∠D + m∠ _____ = 180°

   This is called a _____ angle.

Use the figure to the right to answer each question.

3. If m∠X = 45°, m∠R = _____ °, m∠Y = _____ °,

   and m∠Z = _____ °

4. m∠X + m∠Y = _____ °

5. m∠R + m∠X = _____ °

6. ∠R and ∠X are _____ angles.

Combine each pair of sentences with a conjunction to make a compound sentence.

7. I arrived late for the interview. My alarm clock didn't go off on time. _____

   _____

8. My cousin Jen arrived at six o'clock. We immediately began setting up the

   board game. _____

   _____

9. The restaurant on Colony Road was closed. We ate at the diner across the

   road instead. _____

   _____

10. We have no need to ration the fruit. We have several containers of raspberries

    and cherries. _____

    _____

DAY 16

Read the paragraph. Place an *X* by the logical conclusion. Then, underline the facts that helped you reach this conclusion.

Mrs. Jackson saw an advertisement in the newspaper that read, "Final Sale. All watches $35. Available while supplies last. Cash only." Mrs. Jackson needed cash, so she went to the bank. The ATM was broken, so she completed a withdrawal slip and gave it to the teller. "I'm sorry," the teller said as he looked at his computer screen. "You only have $25 in your account."

_____ Mrs. Jackson bought a watch for $25.

_____ The bank teller was mistaken.

_____ Mrs. Jackson was unable to buy a new watch.

_____ Mrs. Jackson bought a unique clock instead.

Write the letter of each ancient empire, civilization, or dynasty next to the phrase that describes it. Some items will be used more than once.

A.	Ancient Greece	B.	Incan Empire	C.	Mayan Empire
D.	Roman Empire	E.	Tang Dynasty	F.	Babylonian Empire

11. _____ This empire was located in what is now Peru.

12. _____ Its capital was located between the Tigris and Euphrates Rivers.

13. _____ Cuzco, the capital city of this empire, had gardens, paved streets, and stone buildings.

14. _____ The idea of democracy originated with this empire.

15. _____ King Hammurabi created the first set of written laws for this empire.

16. _____ At its peak, it controlled almost all of Europe and parts of Africa.

17. _____ Athens and Sparta were two important city-states of this civilization.

18. _____ It flourished in Central America from about 2600 BC to about AD 900.

19. _____ More than one million people lived in Chang'an, its capital city.

20. _____ This was a period of great cultural achievement in China.

FACTOID: Indonesia has about 13,000 islands, most of which are uninhabited by people.

Use the figure to the right to list all of the pairs of angles that fit each description.

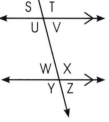

1. alternate exterior angles _____

2. alternate interior angles _____

3. consecutive interior angles_____

4. corresponding angles _____

Use the figure to the right to identify each pair of angles as alternate exterior, alternate interior, consecutive interior, or corresponding.

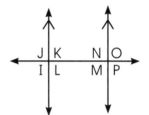

5. ∠I and ∠M are _____ angles.

6. ∠J and ∠P are _____ angles.

7. ∠K and ∠M are _____ angles.

8. ∠L and ∠M are _____ angles.

9. ∠I and ∠O are _____ angles.

10. ∠K and ∠O are _____ angles.

Correlative conjunctions are word pairs that join similar words, phrases, or clauses. The correlative conjunctions are: *both . . . and, neither . . . nor, whether . . . or, either . . . or*, and *not only . . . but* (or *but also*). Write the appropriate correlative conjunctions to complete each sentence.

11. You will need _____ a pencil _____ paper.

12. The toddler drinks _____ milk _____ apple juice.

13. You should ask _____ Rebecca _____ Maria.

14. It is hard to imagine how early scientists worked with _____

    scientific equipment _____ any knowledge of experimentation.

15. _____ Jim _____ Brian asked Krystal to dance.

16. I can't decide _____ I want to see a movie_____ eat dinner.

17. The menu includes _____ Italian _____ French food.

18. _____ come with me, _____ I'll go alone.

DAY 17

Read the passage. Then, answer the questions.

Mustangs

The image of horses running freely across the plains is a popular symbol of the American West. However, mustangs are not **indigenous** to the United States. When Spanish armies came to the New World in the sixteenth century, they brought horses with them. Horses had been extinct in the Western hemisphere for about 12,000 years.

The wild horses that now live in the western part of the United States are called mustangs. The word comes from the Spanish word *mesteño* meaning *wild* or *stray*. The mustangs' ancestors were Spanish horses that had escaped from Spanish soldiers. American Indian tribes also stole and released horses to hurt the Spanish army.

Over many years, the mustang population in western America grew. By the end of the nineteenth century, about two million mustangs roamed the countryside. Farmers and ranchers complained that the mustangs destroyed their crops and ate their livestock's food. Although private conservation efforts began as early as 1925, the mustang population dwindled as many farmers removed the horses from the western plains and prairies. By 1970, fewer than 17,000 mustangs remained in America. In 1971, the U.S. Congress passed a law to protect these wild horses. Today, the government maintains areas that have too many mustangs. Some of the horses are even offered for adoption. About 37,000 mustangs currently live in the United States.

19. Which of the following best defines the word *indigenous*?
    - A. a popular symbol or image
    - B. a breed of wild horse
    - C. native to a particular place
    - D. imported from another country

20. Number the events in the order in which they occurred.
    - _____ About two million mustangs roamed the countryside.
    - _____ Spanish armies brought horses to the New World.
    - _____ Congress passed a law to protect mustangs.
    - _____ Wild horses neared extinction in the Western hemisphere.
    - _____ Private conservation efforts began to protect mustangs.

21. Which of the following statements is true?
    - A. The word *mustang* means free and lovely.
    - B. Mustangs have lived in North America since the end of the last Ice Age.
    - C. The first mustangs in the United States had escaped from the Spanish army.

FITNESS FLASH: Do 10 sit-ups.

* See page ii.

Write the name and number of sides of each figure.

	Name	Number of Sides
1.	_____	_____
2.	_____	_____
3.	_____	_____
4.	_____	_____
5.	_____	_____
6.	_____	_____
7.	_____	_____
8.	_____	_____

An interjection is a word or group of words that expresses emotion. An interjection should be followed by an exclamation point or a comma. Write an interjection to complete each sentence. Then, write two additional sentences that include interjections and appropriate punctuation.

9. _____ I'm not really sure about that.

10. _____ Look at that!

11. _____ Now I understand it better!

12. _____ look! What do you think of this?

13. _____

14. _____

DAY 18

A story's setting tells the time and place of the action. Read each phrase. Write *T* if a phrase indicates time. Write *P* if a phrase indicates place. Then, add a time and a place of your own to the list.

15. _____ after midnight

16. _____ on Tuesday

17. _____ before sundown

18. _____ by the gate

19. _____ in the dead of winter

20. _____ 45 minutes later

21. _____ after the typhoon

22. _____ at twilight

23. _____ in the large cafeteria

24. _____ in the tropics

25. _____ before dawn

26. _____ near the berry patch

27. _____ near the sculpture

28. _____ at the entrance to the theater

29. _____

30. _____

Write the correct word from the word bank for each definition.

| acceleration | friction | inertia | momentum | speed |
| force | gravity | mass | weight | velocity |

31. _____the force that pulls objects toward each other

32. _____ the distance that an object travels in a given time

33. _____the speed in a given direction

34. _____ the force of gravity on an object at a planet's surface

35. _____ the force one object exerts on another when they rub together

36. _____the pushing or pulling on an object

37. _____ the product of an object's mass times its velocity

38. _____the tendency of an object to resist any change in its motion

39. _____ the rate at which an object's velocity changes

40. _____ the amount of matter in an object

FACTOID: The ice at the south pole is about 9,000 feet (2,743 m) thick.

Classify each triangle by examining its angles and sides.

1. _____

2. _____

3. _____

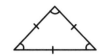

4. _____

5. _____

6. _____

7. _____

8. _____

9. _____

Use the key to identify the part of speech of each underlined word.

ADJ = adjective	CON = conjunction	N = noun	PRO = pronoun
ADV = adverb	INT = interjection	PREP = preposition	V = verb

10. _____ Our class <u>invited</u> all of the middle school students to the festival.

11. _____ <u>Three</u> days each week, I work after school at Kutcher's Office Supply.

12. _____ I've always wanted to earn my <u>degree</u> from our state university.

13. _____ Alfred Hitchcock created many surprise endings in his <u>movies</u>.

14. _____ Sheila wore a sweater <u>under</u> her windbreaker.

15. _____ Finish your homework quickly, <u>and</u> we will watch a movie.

16. _____ Colin entertained <u>us</u> with an excellent portrayal of the villain.

17. _____ Teena bought an <u>absolutely</u> stunning dress at the Oak Street Mall.

18. _____ Portland has a very <u>efficient</u> mass transit system.

19. _____ <u>Wow</u>! Ilena asked me to come to dinner at her house this evening.

20. _____ Ed Chung is one <u>of</u> the greatest athletes to play for Elm High School.

DAY 19

Circle the letter next to the best reference for researching each topic.

21. In which reference would you look for general information about the Mayan culture?
    A. dictionary
    B. atlas
    C. almanac
    D. encyclopedia

22. In which reference would you find a planting chart for different world regions?
    A. atlas
    B. encyclopedia
    C. newspaper
    D. almanac

23. In which reference would you find publication information about a short story?
    A. book of quotations
    B. encyclopedia
    C. literary magazine
    D. newspaper

24. In which reference would you find a word or phrase that means the same as *somber*?
    A. telephone directory
    B. newspaper
    C. encyclopedia
    D. thesaurus

25. In which reference would you find a famous saying from Thomas Edison?
    A. atlas
    B. encyclopedia
    C. book of quotations
    D. almanac

26. In which reference would you find the origin of the word *umbrella*?
    A. dictionary
    B. newspaper
    C. almanac
    D. book of quotations

Think of different fortunes you might read in a fortune cookie. If you could make one fortune come true, what would it be and why? Use another piece of paper if you need more space.

_____

_____

FITNESS FLASH: Do 10 squats.

* See page ii.

Label each type of triangle using a word from the word bank.

| right | obtuse | acute | scalene | isosceles |

1. side lengths are 3 cm, 4 cm, and 6 cm _____

2. angles measure 40°, 60°, and 80° _____

3. angles measure 25°, 10°, and 145° _____

4. side lengths are 6 in., 5 in., and 6 in. _____

5. angles measure 30°, 60°, and 90° _____

Underline the simple subject of each sentence.

6. Marsha filled the vase with water.

7. Relatives gathered at the park for a family reunion.

8. Sarah Bernhardt, famed actress of the early 1900s, continued performing even when confined to a wheelchair.

9. Meteorologist Jimmy Taylor updates us on the weather every evening at 5:00.

10. Dogs, like people, are often very social creatures.

11. A Social Security number is a unique identification number assigned to each citizen of the United States.

12. So far, James Buchanan has been America's only unmarried president.

13. The city of Denver, Colorado, is one mile above sea level.

14. Council members discussed several issues during their July meeting.

15. A white shark can hear sounds up to one mile away.

Read the passage. Then, answer the questions.

Chambered Nautilus

The chambered nautilus is a modern, living fossil. It belongs to a group of mollusks called cephalopods and is related to the octopus, squid, and cuttlefish. Unlike its cousins, the nautilus has an external shell consisting of many chambers. The animal lives in the outermost chamber and uses the rest to regulate its buoyancy, or ability to sink and float. The chambered nautilus lives in the Indian and South Pacific Oceans, finding its home at depths of 900 to 2,000 feet (274 m to 610 m) along reef walls. On dark, moonless nights, it travels closer to the surface to eat tiny fish, shrimp, and the molted shells of spiny lobsters. The chambered nautilus cannot change color or squirt ink like its relatives, but it does have arms. Two rows of 80 to 100 tentacles surround its head. None have suckers to hold prey, but each can touch and taste. The nautilus lives longer than other cephalopods—sometimes up to 20 years. Unlike the octopus, it mates many times during its lifetime, each time attaching its eggs to rocks, coral, or the seafloor. Each egg takes about one year to hatch. Humans are the main threat to this ancient creature's continued survival.

16. Where does the chambered nautilus live? _____

17. Describe the chambered nautilus. _____

   _____

18. What does the chambered nautilus eat? _____

19. What happens to the nautilus's eggs? _____

   _____

20. In the passage, underline a similarity between the chambered nautilus and other cephalopods.

21. In the passage, circle a difference between the chambered nautilus and other cephalopods.

CHARACTER CHECK: Keep a tally throughout the day of the number of times you show respect toward others. Share the results with a family member.

Convection Currents

Boiling water creates currents that rise and sink because of uneven heat. Hot, less dense water rises. As the hot water reaches the surface, it cools and sinks to the bottom of the pot again. This process mimics what molten rocks do within Earth's mantle. These rising and falling movements are called convection currents.

Materials:
- 9" x 13" x 2" (32 cm x 23 cm x 5 cm) clear, glass baking dish that is safe for stovetop cooking
- stovetop
- food coloring
- water
- oven mitts

Procedure:
Fill the baking dish halfway with water. Carefully place the dish on the stovetop. With adult supervision, turn the stove on low. The dish will become hot. Remove the dish from the stovetop. Caution: Wear oven mitts to handle the baking dish. Add a few drops of food coloring to the water in the center of the dish. Observe the movement of the water in the dish. In the chart below, draw a diagram of what happens. Add food coloring to different locations in the dish. Again, draw a diagram of what happens.

Center	Left Side	Right Side

1. Describe the convection currents that occurred as the water heated.

   _____

   _____

2. In your own words, describe what caused the convection currents that occurred in the dish.

   _____

   _____

* See page ii.

BONUS

Engineering for Earthquakes

Engineers who design buildings for earthquake-prone areas must keep the possibility of earthquakes in mind. People can be injured by the total or partial collapse of a building or by glass falling from structures. It would be difficult to create an earthquake-proof building. Instead, engineers create earthquake-resistant buildings that may suffer damage during an earthquake but keep people inside and within the immediate vicinity safe. In this activity, you will build a model of an earthquake-resistant skyscraper.

Materials:
- 8 to 10 building blocks
- dictionary
- craft sticks
- rubber bands
- toothpicks
- yardstick or meterstick

Procedure:
On a table, stack 8 to 10 blocks to create a skyscraper. Draw a picture of the skyscraper in the chart. Hold a dictionary about one yard (one meter) above the table. Drop it onto the table next to the skyscraper to create an "earthquake." Record your observations. Use the blocks and the other building materials to try to create a skyscraper that will resist the shaking caused by the "earthquake." Draw a picture of the new skyscraper in the chart. Then, drop the dictionary on the table again. Record your observations. Include why the first skyscraper toppled and how you altered the second skyscraper to make it earthquake resistant.

Drawing of First Skyscraper	Drawing of New Skyscraper

Effect of First Earthquake	Effect of Second Earthquake

Latitude and Longitude: United States and Canada

Lines of latitude and longitude form an imaginary grid over the Earth to help determine any absolute location. An absolute location is the definitive location of a place using a recognized coordinate system. Relative location is a place's location in relation to nearby places.

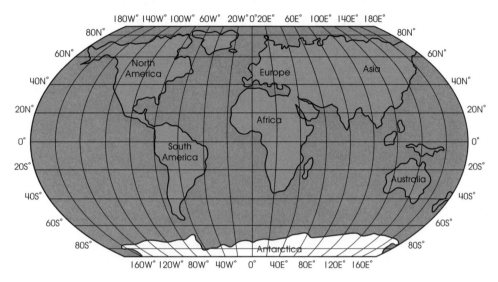

Use an atlas to answer the following questions about locations in the United States and Canada.

1. Which state includes the intersection of 35°N and 120°W? _____

2. Which province is located north of Idaho, east of British Columbia, and west of Saskatchewan? _____

3. Which ocean is includes the intersection of 30°N and 30°W? _____

4. Which state is located north of Florida, east of Alabama, west of the Atlantic Ocean, and southwest of South Carolina? _____

5. Which state includes the intersection of 35°N and 105°W? _____

6. Which ocean includes the intersection of 75°N and 135°W?_____

7. Which mountains cross the 120°W line of longitude?_____

8. Which line of latitude is the border between Nebraska and Kansas? _____

9. Which line of latitude follows the northern border of four provinces? _____

10. Which lines of latitude and longitude intersect in Illinois?_____

11. What line of longitude does the Mississippi River cross?_____

BONUS

The Role of Government

A government can provide services for many of its citizens' needs. Its primary functions involve making, implementing, and enforcing laws and managing any conflicts about laws. A government also provides for the nation's defense.

Match each need on the right with the corresponding government service on the left. More than one government service may meet the same need.

1. _____ education
2. _____ communication
3. _____ safety
4. _____ national defense
5. _____ transportation
6. _____ health
7. _____ help for the needy
8. _____ clean air and water
9. _____ money to trade for goods

A. print money
B. provide a police force
C. build roads
D. provide unemployment benefits
E. fund and staff public schools
F. inspect food and medications
G. deliver mail
H. make laws to restrict pollution
I. fund, staff, and train armed forces

International Services

Research the services that are provided by the United Nations, the World Health Organization, UNICEF, or other international aid organizations. Write a paragraph comparing the services that are offered to the services listed in the activity above.

_____

_____

_____

_____

_____

_____

_____

_____

If Landmarks Could Talk

Some buildings, landmarks, and natural features are so well-known that you may recognize them even if you have never seen them in person. Identify the following places by reading the clues. Then, use reference materials to check your answers.

1. I am a famous attraction in the United States. I am 279 miles (449 km) long and 1 mile (1.6 km) deep. People come from all over the world to hike in and around me.

   _____

2. Built by an emperor as a tomb for his wife, I am one of the most beautiful buildings in the world. I am found about 105 miles (169 km) southeast of New Delhi, India.

   _____

3. I have stood for almost 2,500 years on a hill called the Acropolis. The people of Greece built me to honor the goddess Athena.

   _____

4. Famous for my giant, stone statues of huge heads with long ears, I am found about 2,300 miles (3,700 km) west of Chile in the Pacific Ocean.

   _____

5. Built completely by hand, I am the longest structure ever built. I stretch about 4,000 miles (6,400 km) across northern China.

   _____

6. Located in the largest city in Australia, about 425 miles (684 km) northeast of Melbourne, I stand on the waterfront and look like a giant sailboat.

   _____

7. I was built to house cathedral bells. But, the soil on which I stand is too soft, so I do not stand completely upright. I am found in a city about 42 miles (68 km) west and just south of Florence, Italy.

   _____

8. I am an ancient monument that may have been used as a ceremonial or religious center. I am made of a group of huge stones arranged in a circle on a plain in southwestern England.

   _____

9. I am an enormous limestone statue with the head of a human and the body of a lion. Built about 4,500 years ago in Egypt, I stand 66 feet (20 m) tall, and I am 240 feet (73 m) long.

   _____

10. Erected as a memorial to honor four U.S. presidents, I am carved into a South Dakota mountain.

    _____

BONUS

Take It Outside!

With an adult, take a pen and a notebook outside during the early morning. Write what you see and hear. Reflect on your morning observations. Just before dusk, go outside again with an adult to the same spot. Record the sights and sounds you hear at this time of the day. Then, compare your notes of day and night activity. How do the morning observations compare with what you saw and heard at dusk? Write a poem or essay comparing the two times of day. Create an illustration that captures the mood to accompany the poem or essay.

With family members, visit a local adventure park for a day. Bring a camera and take pictures of various adventure rides. Then, print the pictures and create a collage of the rides. Label each photo to indicate which rides produce thrills with motion or by force. Share your collage and findings with your family and explain how the rides use force and motion.

With a family member, visit different areas in your community. Bring a camera. Look for triangle shapes that have been used in the design or construction of buildings. When you spot a triangle, take a picture. Print the pictures and look for similarities and differences in how the triangles are used. Make a photo album, noting how simple triangle shapes can add character to your community. Tally the number of examples that you found for each type of triangle: equilateral, isosceles, scalene, and right. Which was the hardest to find? Which was the easiest?

Triangle Type	Number of Examples
equilateral	
isosceles	
scalene	
right	

* See page ii.

Monthly Goals

Think of three goals to set for yourself this month. For example, you may want to learn five new vocabulary words each week. Write your goals on the lines. Post them somewhere that you will see them every day.

Draw a check mark beside each goal you meet. Feel proud that you have met your goals and continue to set new ones to challenge yourself.

1. _____

2. _____

3. _____

Word List

The following words are used in this section. Use a dictionary to look up each word that you do not know. Then, write three sentences. Use at least one word from the word list in each sentence.

dynasty	phases
immortalized	quenched
maxim	unison
omitted	verge
pastoral	wrench

1. _____

_____

2. _____

_____

3. _____

_____

Introduction to Endurance

This section includes fitness and character development activities that focus on endurance. These activities are designed to get you moving and thinking about developing your physical and mental stamina.

Physical Endurance

What do climbing stairs, jogging, and riding your bike have in common? They are all great ways to build endurance!

Having endurance means performing an activity for a period of time before your body becomes tired. Improving your endurance requires regular aerobic exercise, which causes your heart to beat faster. You also breathe harder. As a result of regular aerobic activity, your heart becomes stronger, and your blood cells deliver oxygen to your body more efficiently.

Summer provides numerous opportunities to improve your endurance. Although there are times when a relaxing activity is valuable, it is important to take advantage of the warm mornings and sunny days to go outside. Choose activities that you enjoy. Invite a family member to go for a walk or a bike ride. Play a game of basketball with friends. Leave the relaxing activities for when it is dark, too hot, or raining.

Set an endurance goal this summer. For example, you might jog every day until you can run one mile without stopping. Set new goals when you meet your old ones. Be proud of your endurance success!

Mental Endurance

Endurance applies to the mind as well as to the body. Showing mental endurance means persevering. You can show mental endurance every day. Continuing with tasks when you might want to quit and working until they are done are ways that you can show mental endurance.

Build your mental endurance this summer. Maybe you want to earn some extra money for a new bike by helping your neighbors with yard work. But, after one week of working in your neighbors' yards, it is not as easy as you thought it would be. Think about some key points, such as how you have wanted that new bike for months. Be positive. Remind yourself that you have been working for only one week and that your neighbors are very appreciative of your work. Think of ways to make the yard work more enjoyable, such as starting earlier in the day or listening to music while you work. Quitting should be the last resort.

Build your mental endurance now. It will help prepare you for challenges you may face later.

Find each missing angle measurement or side length.

1.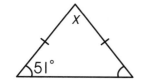

_____

2.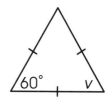

_____

3.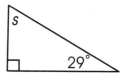

_____

4.

_____

5.

_____

6.

_____

A compound subject contains two or more simple subjects that have the same verb or verb phrase. Circle the compound subject in each sentence.

7. Swimming, fishing, hiking, and horseback riding are all offered at El Conquistador Resort in Phoenix, Arizona.

8. Iced tea, iced coffee, lemonade, and cold soft drinks are always available at the swimming pool's concession stand.

9. Cindy, Stephanie, and Jeanine spent much of their time together last summer swimming in Walton Lake.

10. Grover and Linda Flowers flew to Tallahassee, Florida, to be with their daughter Heather during Parents' Weekend.

11. Firefighters and police officers hold dangerous jobs.

12. Tents, sleeping bags, cooking utensils, and other camping gear are stored in the Boy Scout meeting house.

13. Orange roughy, halibut, and swordfish are all seafood entrées on the menu at Skipper's Galley.

14. Benji, Eric, and Winston have been friends since second grade.

DAY 1

Read each word. Write the root word, the prefix, and the suffix in the correct columns. Some words will have either a prefix or a suffix, and some words may have both a prefix and a suffix.

	Prefix	Root Word	Suffix
15. expressible			
16. unbelievable			
17. dramatize			
18. allowance			
19. researcher			

The chart compares currency exchange rates between U.S. dollars and several other currencies.

Currencies	What the Currency Equals in U.S. Dollars	What US$1 Equals in the Currency
Canadian dollar	$1.03	0.974 Canadian dollars
Russian ruble	$0.04	27.84 rubles
Japanese yen	$0.0127	78.95 yen
Indian rupee	$0.0224	44.56 rupees

20. Complete the chart to find the cost of a soft drink in U.S. dollars in each country. The first one has been done for you.

Your $5	×	What US$1 Equals in the Currency	=	What US$5 Equals in the Currency	−	Cost of a Soft Drink in the Currency	=	Your Change in the Currency	×	What the Currency Equals in U.S. Dollars	=	Your Change in U.S. Dollars	Cost of a Soft Drink in U.S. Dollars
A. US$5	×	0.974 dollars (Canadian)	=	4.87 dollars (Canadian)	−	1.35 dollars (Canadian)	=	3.52 dollars (Canadian)	×	$1.03	=	$3.63	$1.37
B. US$5	×	27.84 rubles	=	____ rubles	−	35 rubles	=	____ rubles	×	$0.04	=	$4.17	$_____
C. US$5	×	78.95 yen	=	268.73 yen	−	120 yen	=	____ yen	×	$0.0127	=	$1.89	$_____
D. US$5	×	44.56 rupees	=	222.80 rupees	−	150 rupees	=	72.80 rupees	×	$0.0224	=	$_____	$_____

FACTOID: The Peregrine falcon can dive at a speed of 200 miles per hour.

Use the Pythagorean theorem to find each missing side length. Round to the nearest hundredth.

1.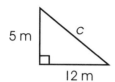

2.

3.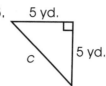

4.

_____   _____   _____   _____

5.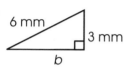

6.

7.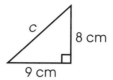

8.

_____   _____   _____   _____

A compound predicate contains two or more separate verbs that refer to the same subject. Circle the compound verbs in each sentence.

9.   Coach Smith walked to the podium and smiled at the stadium of cheering fans.

10. A good salesperson knows failure but can turn some failures into successes.

11. Tony sprinted from second base and slid into third.

12. I ordered popcorn and a soft drink and then decided to have juice instead.

13. Van passed the ball to Cramer and ran down the field.

14. The entire class stayed after school and cleaned the stage.

15. While vacationing, I liked the sights, sounds, and smells of the city and enjoyed the people there.

16. Scientists studied the diamondback rattlesnake and recorded their observations.

17. The large ape pounded his chest and roared loudly.

18. Jeff bought a farm and built a new house in the same year.

19. Corinne birdied the eighth hole but bogeyed the ninth.

20. The insurance company paid for the damage to Tim's car but withheld his $250 deductible from the total invoice.

DAY 2

Circle the answer that correctly completes each analogy.

21. poet: verses :: _____
    - A. cooper: shoes
    - B. cobbler: hats
    - C. novelist: music
    - D. cartographer: maps

22. virtuoso: mediocre :: _____
    - A. novice: inexperienced
    - B. talented: gifted
    - C. recluse: sociable
    - D. nomad: itinerant

23. valiant: courage :: _____
    - A. chipper: melancholy
    - B. wrathful: boredom
    - C. tyrannical: power
    - D. frightened: effrontery

24. dexterity: nimble :: _____
    - A. integrity: duplicitous
    - B. complacent: eager
    - C. novel: pamphlet
    - D. hubris: arrogance

25. gale: wind :: _____
    - A. deluge: rain
    - B. snow: blizzard
    - C. flood: tidal wave
    - D. frostbite: cold

26. apple: tree :: _____
    - A. fruit: vegetable
    - B. grape: vine
    - C. plum: pear
    - D. banana: peel

You have just been hired as a reporter for the *Way Out There* world newspaper, specializing in unique and wacky news. Create a headline for your first news story. Then, write the news story to accompany your headline. You may quote imaginary scientists, authorities, or other sources. Use another piece of paper if you need more space.

_____

_____

_____

_____

_____

_____

FITNESS FLASH: Jog in place for 30 seconds.

* See page ii.

Find the radius of each circle.

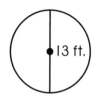

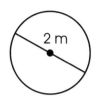

1. _____ 2. _____ 3. _____ 4. _____

Find the diameter of each circle.

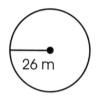

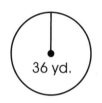

5. _____ 6. _____ 7. _____ 8. _____

A simple sentence, or independent clause, contains a subject and a predicate and expresses a complete thought. A compound sentence contains two simple sentences joined by a conjunction. Read each sentence. Write *S* if the sentence is simple. Write *C* if the sentence is compound.

9. _____ Luke goes home and studies every day after school.

10. _____ Alyson and her sister Samantha have completely different interests.

11. _____ The telephone rang, and the doorbell buzzed at the same time.

12. _____ Both the canoe and the sailboat belong to Uncle Bill and Aunt Nancy.

13. _____ You bring the sandwiches, and I'll bring the chips and fruit.

14. _____ Lesley Mitchell finished her project ahead of schedule, but she didn't submit it to her English teacher until the due date.

15. _____ You should get your bike and join our trip.

16. _____ Many of the early settlers had never been farmers, and they were not prepared for the harsh New England winters.

17. _____ Camilla stayed longer than usual.

18. _____ Really great movies are hard to find, but I'm not very picky.

DAY 3

Read the passage. Then, answer the questions.

Taking a Poll

A poll is a survey of random opinions to be analyzed for a specific purpose. A classroom poll might ask students to name their favorite foods or their favorite musical groups. The polling question should always be neutral so that the results are not biased. This means that the question must not influence the answer. For example, the question, *I do not like pizza, do you?* may bias the respondent to agree with the question instead of provide a true opinion. Large groups can be polled by using a subsample, or smaller representative group, instead of polling every person. The subsample should be chosen at random. To find out which sport eighth-graders at your local middle school like best, you might make a list of their names and ask every third person for an opinion. However, if you polled only eighth-graders at the park, your sample might be biased toward people who already play sports there.

19. What is the main idea of this passage?
    A. People who like sports often go to the park.
    B. You can take a poll to learn about people's favorite foods.
    C. A poll should be unbiased and include a random sample.

20. What does it mean to conduct an unbiased poll?
    A. to visit the park and ask people their favorite sport
    B. to ask a question in a way that does not influence the people who are answering
    C. to talk to only eighth graders about their favorite sports

21. What is an unbiased way of asking the polling question about sports in the passage? _____

    _____

22. What is a *subsample*? _____

    _____

23. How can a large group of people be polled without talking to every person?

    _____

FACTOID: The average summer temperature in Antarctica is 35.6°F (2°C).

Find the area and perimeter of each figure. Show your work on a separate sheet of paper.

1. 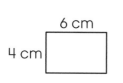 6 cm, 4 cm	2. 12 in.	3. 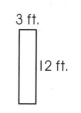 3 ft., 12 ft.
A=_____ P=_____	A=_____ P=_____	A=_____ P=_____
4. 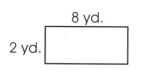 8 yd., 2 yd.	5. 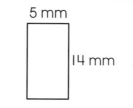 5 mm, 14 mm	6. 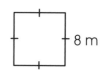 8 m
A=_____ P=_____	A=_____ P=_____	A=_____ P=_____
7. 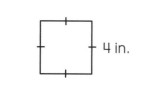 4 in.	8. 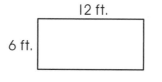 12 ft., 6 ft.	9. 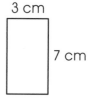 3 cm, 7 cm
A=_____ P=_____	A=_____ P=_____	A=_____ P=_____

An independent clause expresses a complete thought. A dependent clause has a subject and a verb but does not express a complete thought. Read each clause. Write *I* if it is an independent clause. Write *D* if it is a dependent clause.

10. _____ When Buster grew tired of chasing after the ball

11. _____ She was not fearful of the dentist during her checkup this year

12. _____ I have a great deal of respect for people with character

13. _____ Because she cannot help crying at sad movies

Circle each independent clause and underline each dependent clause.

14. I want to be the first to volunteer whenever the teacher asks for help.

15. If you stay until the birthday party is over, call Mom for a ride home.

16. When monsoon season begins, the humidity makes the air uncomfortable.

17. Pizza is Crawford's choice for dinner, but only if it has a thin crust.

DAY 4

Read each sentence. Use context clues to match each boldfaced word with its definition.

18. _____ My uncle used a hammer to **wrench** the nail from the board.

19. _____ Daniel auditioned for a **role** in the school play.

20. _____ Silk has a very smooth **texture**.

21. _____ Our class answered the question in **unison**.

22. _____ The teacher accidentally **omitted** Cathy's name from the list.

23. _____ We learned about the **phases** of the moon in science class.

24. _____ Tony **quenched** his thirst after the race by drinking water.

25. _____ Scientists believed that they were on the **verge** of finding a cure for the disease.

26. _____ "Actions speak louder than words" is an old **maxim**.

A. a part played by an actor

B. at the edge

C. general rule or truth

D. left out

E. stages

F. satisfied

G. at the same time

H. pull out

I. characteristics of a surface

Make Endurance Routine!

Endurance is the ability to perform a physical activity for an extended period of time. There are many ways to build endurance. For this activity, you will need a jump rope and a stopwatch.

To begin, walk briskly in place for two minutes to warm up. Then, jog in place for one minute. Jump rope for two minutes and do jumping jacks for one minute. To cool down and complete your routine, walk in place for one minute. Catch your breath. Repeat this activity if possible, or set an endurance goal for completing this activity.

To make this activity more challenging, gradually increase the length of each exercise and change the order of the activities.

FITNESS FLASH: Do 10 jumping jacks.

* See page ii.

Find the area and perimeter of each polygon. Show your work on a separate sheet of paper.

1.

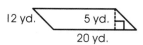

A= _____ P= _____

2.

A= _____ P= _____

3.

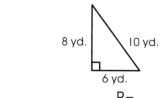

A= _____ P= _____

4.

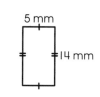

A= _____ P= _____

5.

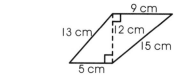

A= _____ P= _____

6.

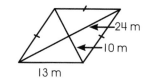

A= _____ P= _____

7.

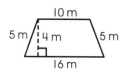

A= _____ P= _____

8.

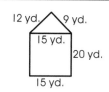

A= _____ P= _____

A complex sentence contains one independent clause and one or more dependent clauses. Underline each independent clause and circle each dependent clause.

9.   We stopped playing and sought shelter when the storm began.

10. Gabe hopped off his skateboard so that his friend could use it.

11. We won the state championship because we played together as a team.

12. Although the price of gasoline rose by 50 cents per gallon, Americans did not curb their travel plans.

13. If we fail to finish our project tonight, we will not be in Mrs. Hooper's good graces tomorrow.

DAY 5

Jargon is an expression directed at a specialized audience, such as sports fans. Slang is informal language that may be inappropriate for some occasions or may become quickly outdated. Avoid jargon and slang when writing for a general audience.

Read each sentence. Circle the jargon or slang. Write words that better express the jargon or slang.

14. Jake said that the group's new song was off the hook. _____

15. "I read it twice," said Mark. "But, I still don't get it." _____

16. Bert gave me props for my high score on the test. _____

17. "What's up?" asked Dr. Marvel as he greeted his students. _____

18. The dress Suzie wore is really in right now. _____

19. The Morton family wanted to chill, so they stayed home all weekend and rested.

    _____

20. Tammy studied for the physics exam for so long that she knew she would hit it out of the park.

    _____

Write the letter of the word from the word bank that matches each definition.

A. producer	B. consumer	C. decomposer	D. carnivore
E. scavenger	F. herbivore	G. omnivore	

21. _____ an organism that breaks down dead organisms and waste

22. _____ an organism that cannot create its own food, so it eats other organisms

23. _____ an organism that eats the remains of dead animals

24. _____ an organism that eats only plants

25. _____ an organism that eats both plants and animals

26. _____ an organism that creates its own food through photosynthesis

27. _____ an organism that eats only animals

CHARACTER CHECK: What does *perseverance* mean? Write about a time when you showed perseverance.

Find the area and perimeter of each triangle. Show your work on a separate sheet of paper.

1.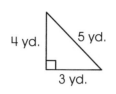

   A=_____ P=_____

2.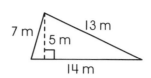

   A=_____ P=_____

3.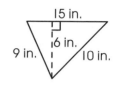

   A=_____ P=_____

4.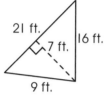

   A=_____ P=_____

5.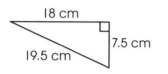

   A=_____ P=_____

6.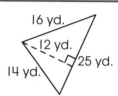

   A=_____ P=_____

7.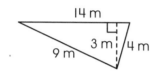

   A=_____ P=_____

8.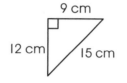

   A=_____ P=_____

9.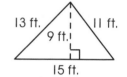

   A=_____ P=_____

Read each group of words. Write _C_ if the group of words is a complete sentence. Write _F_ if the group of words is a sentence fragment.

10. _____ Kelly and the red balloon

11. _____ Although a former soldier and a member of Congress

12. _____ After finding the answer to her question, Coleen printed the story as proof

13. _____ Fell coming out of the starting block but made up lots of ground

14. _____ Unless you buy a ticket

15. _____ Many of my friends love to play video games

16. _____ Who would have had a clue that he would win

Write a complete sentence using this sentence fragment.

17. Until the end of the semester _____

_____

DAY 6

Read the passage. Then, answer the questions.

The Ides of March

William Shakespeare **immortalized** the phrase, *the ides of March*. In Shakespeare's play, *Julius Caesar*, Caesar asks a soothsayer, or fortune teller, what his future holds. Caesar is told, "Beware the ides of March!" It is a phrase that is still used today.

The *ides of March* means the *15th of March*. The Roman calendar built its months around three types of days: calends (the 1st day of the month), nones (the 7th day of the month), and ides (either the 13th or 15th day of the month). In some months, the ides fell on the 15th day of the month. In other months, the ides fell on the 13th day. Romans identified the other days of the month by counting backward or forward from the calends, nones, or ides. For example, the 18th day of a month would be three days after the ides. Every month had an ides, but the ides of March has historical significance because Julius Caesar was assassinated in 44 BC on the 15th of March.

Aside from the ides of March, the Romans provided the basis for our modern-day calendar system of 365.25 days per year and 366 days during a leap year. The Romans also gave us the word *calendar*, which originates from their word *calends*. So, we have Shakespeare and the Ancient Romans to thank for the term *ides of March*.

18. On which day of the month might the ides fall?
    A. the 1st day of the month
    B. the 7th day of the month
    C. the last day of the month
    D. the 15th day of the month

19. Which of the following best defines the word *immortalized*?
    A. explained clearly
    B. accented
    C. made to last forever
    D. to tell the future

20. In Shakespeare's play, why did the soothsayer tell Caesar, "Beware the ides of March"?
    A. He was predicting Caesar's assassination.
    B. He had met Caesar, and he did not like him.
    C. He was addressing a very important man.

21. Which best summarizes the main idea of this passage?
    A. The Roman calendar only had three days.
    B. Julius Caesar was assassinated on the ides of March.
    C. The *ides of March* is a popular term because of Shakespeare's *Julius Caesar*.

FACTOID: Two stars that orbit each other are called doubles. About half of the stars in the universe are doubles.

Find the surface area of each rectangular prism. Show your work on a separate sheet of paper.

1.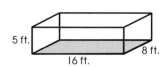

SA = _____

2.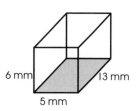

SA = _____

3.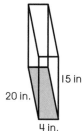

SA = _____

4.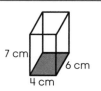

SA = _____

5.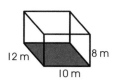

SA = _____

6.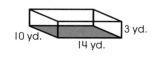

SA = _____

A run-on sentence occurs when two or more independent clauses are not properly connected. Rewrite each run-on sentence to form one correct sentence.

7. Colin's dad is the CEO of First Federal Bank he is also the bank's president.

_____

8. Our cat, Coz, jumped from the patio to the wall he was afraid to jump down the other side into an unfamiliar place. _____

_____

_____

9. Lisa lives an active life she is the busiest person I've ever met. _____

_____

10. Ms. Crawford's explanation didn't make sense to Ellie she solved the math problem her own way. _____

_____

DAY 7

Read the passage. What conclusion can you draw about Jon's future education? Write your conclusion. Use a separate piece of paper if you need more space.

Jon was worried. He anticipated that the envelope would arrive in the mail that day. If the envelope was large, it meant that he was accepted to the college of his choice. He reasoned that a large envelope meant that there were many forms to complete as part of the registration process. On the other hand, a small envelope might mean bad news. A small envelope meant that it held only one piece of paper—a letter indicating that he was not accepted.

Just then, the doorbell rang. "Delivery," announced Mr. Foxman, the mail carrier. Jon raced to the door. "Gee," said Mr. Foxman, handing Jon the envelope, "they needed extra postage for this one."

_____

_____

Write the letter of each U.S. document next to its description.

11. _____ defined the rights of U.S. citizens in relation to the Constitution

12. _____ allowed the United States to purchase the land west of the Mississippi River from France

13. _____ four-page document, which was signed in 1787, established the U.S. government

14. _____ closed colonization of the Western Hemisphere

15. _____ served as the first U.S. Constitution

16. _____ issued by President Lincoln during the Civil War, it freed all slaves in the Confederate states

17. _____ provided a method for admitting new states into the country

18. _____ stated that the 13 original colonies were no longer subject to British rule

A. Declaration of Independence

B. Articles of Confederation

C. Northwest Ordinance

D. Monroe Doctrine

E. Bill of Rights

F. Louisiana Purchase Treaty

G. U.S. Constitution

H. Emancipation Proclamation

FITNESS FLASH: Hop on your left foot 10 times.

* See page ii.

Find the volume of each solid. Round to the nearest hundredth. Show your work on a separate sheet of paper.

1.

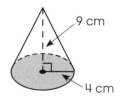

9 cm

4 cm

V = _____

2.

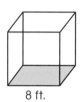

8 ft.

V = _____

3.

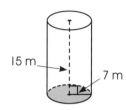

15 m

7 m

V = _____

4.

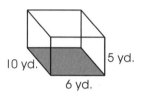

10 yd.

5 yd.

6 yd.

V = _____

5.

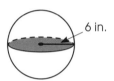

6 in.

V = _____

6.

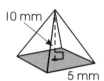

10 mm

5 mm

V = _____

Varying the lengths of your sentences will help maintain your reader's attention. Combine each sentence pair into a single sentence that retains all important information.

7. Kelly worked for years as a consultant for Harnquist and Beckman. She now has her own consulting firm. _____

_____

8. Lake Powell occupies parts of both Arizona and Utah. It is the largest lake in either state. _____

_____

9. We had box seats in the front row. We could put our drinks on top of the Cardinal's dugout. _____

_____

DAY 8

Look closely at the context of each sentence to determine the correct word choice. Then, circle the word that correctly completes each sentence. Use a dictionary if needed.

10. Everyone was able to attend the concert (accept, except) Raymond, who had a previous commitment.

11. Hilda's great-grandparents had (immigrated, emigrated) to the United States from Sweden in the early 1900s.

12. When (its, it's) time to go, we can call the restaurant for an advance reservation.

13. Tokens for the subway (fare, fair) can be purchased in coin-operated machines outside the station.

14. We first brought the towels into the house, (than, then) we folded them and put them away.

15. (There, They're, Their) house on Cherry Street has always been the most majestic old home in all of Gladstone.

16. (Whose, Who's) golf club is this?

17. Manny and Mario have (to, two, too) pet turtles in their room.

18. Mrs. Sherman has been our (principle, principal) for the last two years.

19. When you walk (past, passed) the cafeteria, please check the menu for today's lunch.

20. I am looking for a CD (that, which) has a collection of jazz music.

Select one or two characters, one location, and one event. On a separate piece of paper, use them to write a creative and detailed story.

Characters: talking earthworm, clown, out-of-control robot, princess, teacher, principal

Locations: school, amusement park, boat, airplane, shopping mall, basement

Events: yelling, smelling something unusual, running backward, sneezing, talking while asleep, falling from the sky

FACTOID: Thomas Jefferson spoke six languages.

Name the congruent angles of each reflection.

1. ∠RQS ≅ ∠ _____; ∠QRS ≅ ∠ _____;
   ∠QSR ≅ ∠ _____

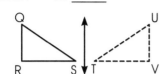

2. ∠ _____ ≅ ∠ _____; ∠ _____ ≅ ∠ _____;
   ∠ _____ ≅ ∠ _____; ∠ _____ ≅ ∠ _____;
   ∠ _____ ≅ ∠ _____

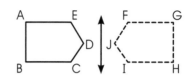

Name the congruent angles of each translation.

3. ∠ABC ≅ ∠ _____; ∠BCD ≅ ∠ _____;
   ∠CDA ≅ ∠ _____; ∠DAB ≅ ∠ _____

4. ∠ _____ ≅ ∠ _____;
   ∠ _____ ≅ ∠ _____;
   ∠ _____ ≅ ∠ _____;
   ∠ _____ ≅ ∠ _____;
   ∠ _____ ≅ ∠ _____;

Name the congruent angles of each rotation.

5. ∠ _____ ≅ ∠ _____; ∠ _____ ≅ ∠ _____;
   ∠ _____ ≅ ∠ _____

6. ∠ _____ ≅ ∠ _____; ∠ _____ ≅ ∠ _____;
   ∠ _____ ≅ ∠ _____; ∠ _____ ≅ ∠ _____

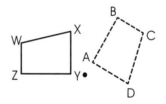

Circle the word that correctly completes each sentence.

7. Gretchen gave Mrs. Cooke a gift and (than, then) told her that she was her favorite teacher.

8. Lance Armstrong's seventh Tour de France win, (that, which) happened in 2005, set a new record.

9. (Your, You're) being late for practice cost our team valuable preparation time.

10. The club (that, which) hosted this year's tournament was in Wisconsin.

11. If you don't know where (your, you're) going, how will you know when you get there?

DAY 9

Read the selection. Then, answer the questions.

Much of Robert Frost's work, like this **pastoral** poem, describes the life and landscapes of rural New England, where he spent much of his life.

Going for Water by Robert Frost

The well was dry beside the door
And so we went with pail and can
Across the fields behind the house
To seek the brook if still it ran;
Not loth to have excuse to go,   5
Because the autumn eve was fair
(Though chill), because the fields were ours,
And by the brook our woods were there.
We ran as if to meet the moon
That slowly dawned behind the trees,   10
The barren boughs without the leaves,
Without the birds, without the breeze.
But once within the wood, we paused
Like gnomes that hid us from the moon,
Ready to run to hiding new   15
With laughter when she found us soon.
Each laid on other a staying hand
To listen ere we dared to look,
And in the hush we joined to make
We heard, we knew we heard the brook.   20
A note as from a single place,
A slender tinkling fall that made
Now drops that floated on the pool
Like pearls, and now a silver blade.

12.   What does *pastoral* mean? Which words in the poem support this description?

_____

13.   Based on the poem's tone, how do the characters feel about fetching the water?

_____

14.   In line 16, who does *she* refer to? _____

FITNESS FLASH: Hop on your right foot for 30 seconds.

* See page ii.

Draw the rotation of each figure.

1. 180° rotation

 .

2. 135° rotation

 .

3. 45° rotation

.

4. 90° counterclockwise rotation

 .

Proper grammar avoids the use of two negatives in the same clause because the result can be awkward and confusing. Rewrite each sentence to correct the double negative.

5. Kelly doesn't want no more interruptions.

_____

_____

6. Kim Tracie never did nothing wrong until she broke her mother's favorite vase.

_____

_____

7. Dr. Canberra was born in Argentina, but he never traveled nowhere else once he arrived in the United States.

_____

_____

8. I left home without my umbrella since there is not no chance of rain today.

_____

_____

DAY 10

Read each sentence. Write *F* if the sentence is written from the first-person point of view. Write *T* if the sentence is written from the third-person point of view. Then, write a sentence in first person about your favorite sport or hobby.

9. _____ When I saw the size of the gift box, I knew it was the bike I had wanted.

10. _____ Struggling with the humid air, they slowed their pace and rested in a crevice near the rock.

11. _____ The travelers finished packing their bags and headed for the airport.

12. _____ He delivered the newspapers that morning to a total of 96 homes.

13. _____ By morning, I had written the last chapter of my 234-page novel.

14. _____ Despite the low price, I still expect a discount on the draperies.

15. _____ She knows the names of her state senators and representatives.

16. _____

_____

Match each characteristic of metal with its description.

| malleable | ductile | conductor | magnetic | reactivity | alloy |

17. able to be pulled into long wires _____

18. able to be pounded and hammered into different shapes _____

19. a combination of two or more metals _____

20. the ease and speed with which an element combines with other elements and compounds _____

21. a metal that transmits heat and electricity _____

22. the ability to attract other metallic objects _____

CHARACTER CHECK: Make a list of at least three ways you can show tolerance at home and at school. Post the list somewhere visible.

Determine whether each figure or shape has been dilated and write *yes* or *no*. Then, explain your answer by writing *reduced*, *expanded*, or *neither*.

	Dilated	**Explanation**
1.	_____	_____
2.	_____	_____
3.	_____	_____
4.	_____	_____
5.	_____	_____
6.	_____	_____
7.	_____	_____
8.	_____	_____

Read each sentence. Draw three lines under each letter that should be capitalized.

9. who originally said, "haste makes waste"?

10. we bought a beautiful american indian mosaic rug in arizona.

11. tacos are lindsey's favorite mexican food.

12. there are many giant redwood trees in sequoia national park.

13. the second sunday in may is always mother's day in the united states.

14. if you close the blinds in your living room, you will gain more privacy.

15. our school year at roosevelt middle school usually begins on the wednesday before labor day.

DAY II

Read the paragraph. Circle the letter of the sentence that states the main idea. Then, underline three supporting details.

The world's tropical rain forests are in great danger. Loggers cut down trees to provide timber and firewood and make room for homes, roads, farms, and factories. Some areas are cleared to mine oil and other valuable minerals. The habitats of thousands of animal and plant species have already vanished. These changes also threaten the way of life for many native residents.

A. Tropical rain forests contain an incredible amount of plant and animal diversity.

B. Tropical rain forests are in great danger.

C. Tropical rain forests are located near the equator.

Read the passage. Then, answer the questions.

The U.S. Government

The U.S. government consists of three separate branches: executive, legislative, and judicial. The president, vice president, and the cabinet of advisors represent the executive branch. The president, elected by the people, chooses the cabinet, subject to Senate approval. The Senate and House of Representatives form the U.S. Congress in the legislative branch. Each state elects two senators. Senators' six-year terms are staggered so that only one-third of the Senate is elected every two years. Each state also elects a designated number of representatives, determined by state population. The House of Representatives contains 435 members. All representatives are elected every two years. The third branch of the U.S. government is the judicial branch, which consists of courts of law throughout the nation. The highest court is the Supreme Court, containing nine justices. When a justice's seat opens, the president nominates a candidate who must be approved by the Senate.

16. What is the main idea of this passage?

    A. The Senate approves the president's cabinet choices.

    B. The president and members of Congress are elected.

    C. The U.S. government contains three separate branches.

17. Which offices form the executive branch? _____

18. Which groups represent the U.S. Congress? _____

> **FACTOID:** The first successful helicopter flight occurred in 1906. Its time off the ground was 20 seconds.

Use each scale factor to determine whether the dilation is an enlargement or a reduction.

1. SF = $\dfrac{1}{2}$ _____

2. SF = 120% _____

3. SF = $\dfrac{8}{9}$ _____

4. SF = 32% _____

5. SF = 4 _____

6. SF = $\dfrac{2}{3}$ _____

7. SF = 247% _____

8. SF = 8 _____

Find the scale factor in each dilation.

9. 12 in. 12 in. 12 in. 12 in.   9 in. 9 in. 9 in. 9 in.

    SF = _____

10.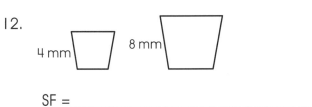

    SF = _____

11. 14 ft. 21 ft.

    SF = _____

12. 4 mm   8 mm

    SF = _____

Read each sentence. Draw three lines under each letter that should be capitalized.

13. col. carlson and his unit served breakfast for the husbands and wives of american soldiers who are serving their country.

14. *beauty and the beast* is found in many fairy tale collections.

15. i enjoy going to my grandmother's house for the great meals she prepares every sunday at noon.

16. mom and dad met while on a vacation in historic williamsburg, virginia.

17. eleanor roosevelt said, "no one can make you feel inferior without your consent."

18. the economic differences between the north and the south also played a part in the civil war.

19. the secretary-general of the united nations has a very demanding job.

DAY 12

Read the passage. Then, answer the questions.

Halley's Comet

Halley's Comet was named for its discoverer, astronomer Edmond Halley. Halley theorized that comets were natural **phenomena** of the solar system that traveled in orbits around the sun. He maintained that one specific comet would take 76 years to complete its orbit. After researching sightings in the years 1531, 1607, and 1682, Halley predicted that the comet would return in 1758. His prediction was accurate, and the comet was named in his honor, 16 years after his death. Since that time, Halley's Comet has made regular visits to Earth's orbit about every 76 years. Various forces combine to keep the orbit consistent. However, the gravitational pull of the planets sometimes changes the orbital period. There have been times when the comet's orbit has taken as long as 79 years.

Astronomers have researched the composition of comets. In 1985, the spacecraft *Giotto* was launched to photograph Halley's Comet as it passed Earth. The pictures were taken from 370 miles (600 km) away, the closest distance at which the comet has been monitored. *Giotto* sent valuable data to astronomers. Measurements showed that the comet's nucleus is approximately 9 miles (15 km) in diameter. The dark and porous nucleus is composed of dust that remained after ice changed into a gaseous state. Halley's Comet is scheduled to pass by Earth again in 2061.

20. Which of the following reasons makes Halley's Comet the best-known comet?
    A. the size of its nucleus
    B. its fairly regular orbital pattern
    C. its composition of ice turned to dust
    D. its beauty

21. How often does Halley's Comet pass by Earth?
    A. approximately every 76 years
    B. usually every 89 years
    C. cannot be predicted
    D. once every other century

22. What is the approximate size of the nucleus of Halley's Comet?_____

23. Which of the following best defines the word *phenomena*?
    A. a comet with a predictable orbit
    B. observable, unusual facts or events
    C. routine conditioning
    D. beyond expectation

24. What causes the orbit of Halley's Comet to vary slightly in duration?

_____

FITNESS FLASH: Jog in place for 30 seconds.

* See page ii.

The charts show relationships between some standard measurements for length, weight, and capacity. To convert a smaller unit to a larger unit, divide. To convert a larger unit to a smaller unit, multiply.

Standard Units of Length
12 inches (in.) = 1 foot (ft.)
3 ft. = 1 yard (yd.)
36 in. = 1 yd.
5,280 ft. = 1 mile (mi.)
1,760 yd. = 1 mi.

1.   2 mi. = _____ ft.

2.   1 ft., 3 in. = _____ in.

3.   4 yd. = _____ ft.

4.   60 in. = _____ ft.

5.   5,280 yd. = _____ mi.

6.   144 in. = _____ yd.

Write each equivalent measurement.

Metric Units of Length
10 millimeters (mm) = 1 centimeter (cm)
10 cm = 1 decimeter (dm)
10 dm = 1 meter (m)
10 m = 1 dekameter (dam)
10 dam = 1 hectometer (hm)
10 hm = 1 kilometer (km)

7.   7 m = _____ cm

8.   6 m = _____ dm

9.   3,500 cm = _____ m

10. 82 dm = _____ cm

11. 8 km = _____ m

12. 19,000 m = _____ km

Read the passage. Draw three lines under each letter that should be capitalized.

Spanish Exploration

Spanish explorer Juan Ponce de León first sighted north america on easter sunday in 1513. He claimed the land for Spain and named it La florida, meaning *The Land of the Flowers.*

Spain made attempts to build settlements in florida, but all were failures. Then, king phillip II commissioned Pedro Menendez de Aviles to colonize Florida and drive out any pirates or settlers from other nations.

When menendez arrived in florida in 1565, he, his soldiers, and 500 colonists landed near the american indian village of seloy. Menendez and his men built a fort with the help of some american indians and named the new settlement st. augustine.

DAY 13

Organize the words from the word bank using the outline below.

cows	mammals	frogs	salamanders	amphibians
animals	cardinals	lions	birds	robins
crocodiles	vertebrates	reptiles	snakes	

I. _____

A. _____

    1. _____

        a. _____

        b. _____

    2. _____

        a. _____

        b. _____

    3. _____

        a. _____

        b. _____

    4. _____

        a. _____

        b. _____

A Persevering Attitude

Perseverance means *the action of continuing, even if a task is difficult.* Think about perseverance. When have you seen people demonstrating this quality? What were they doing? What were they hoping to accomplish? Read the situations below. Select one situation. Then, draw a three-panel comic strip showing the before, during, and after. Be sure to include a caption for each panel to describe your persevering attitude.

- You have recently adopted a puppy. The puppy is very energetic and playful. At first, its actions are cute; however, as the puppy grows, you realize that the puppy needs to be trained. You know that teaching the puppy good habits will take perseverance on your part.

- You just found a great summer camp that offers all of the activities that you most enjoy. Your best friend is going, and you want to go too. Your family informs you that you will need to pay for some of the expenses. It is a lot of money to save in a short period of time, but you decide to persevere and make the effort to save the necessary money.

FACTOID: The word *salary* comes from the Latin word *sal*, which means *salt*. Roman soldiers were paid an allowance to buy salt.

Metric Units of Weight
10 milligrams (mg) = 1 centigram (cg)
10 cg = 1 decigram (dg)
10 dg = 1 gram (g)
10 g = 1 dekagram (dag)
10 dag = 1 hectogram (hg)
10 hg = 1 kilogram (kg)

Standard Units of Weight
16 ounces (oz.) = 1 pound (lb.)
2,000 lb. = 1 ton (tn.)

Write each equivalent measurement.

1. 96 oz. = _____ lb.
2. 3 g = _____ kg
3. 3 lb. = _____ oz.
4. 45 dag = _____ g
5. 22 pt. = _____ oz.
6. 66,000 mg = _____ g
7. 2 qt. = _____ oz.
8. 4 kg = _____ mg
9. 9 lb., 3 oz. = _____ oz.
10. 708 mg = _____ dg
11. 10,000 lb. = _____ tn.
12. 35 kg = _____ g
13. 32,000 oz. = _____ tn.
14. 1,000 lb. = _____ tn.

Add commas where they are needed in each sentence.

15. Angie tossed broccoli tomatoes and cauliflower into her salad.

16. Tyler if you will help me roll the dough you can sample some cookies when they are done.

17. Mr. Troute the counselor at our middle school forgot that we scheduled an appointment this morning.

18. Before we start the game we need to read the rules.

19. You will need to bring the hot dogs and buns and I will bring everything else.

20. Since the weather forecaster predicted rain the girls decided to change their afternoon plans.

DAY 14

Persuasive writing is meant to influence the reader to agree with a belief, a position, or a course of action. Expository writing provides information or explains something that may be difficult to understand. Narrative writing describes an event or tells a story.

Read each description. Write _P_ for persuasive, _E_ for expository, or _N_ for narrative to indicate the type of writing.

21. _____ a story about martians in a science fiction magazine

22. _____ the history of how Thomas Edison invented the lightbulb

23. _____ a letter published in a newspaper that encourages voters to support arts education in schools

Write the word from the word bank that matches each description.

gasohol	geothermal	hydroelectric	solar
nuclear	biomass	wind	

24. _____ energy produced by atomic reactions

25. _____ energy collected from the sun's radiation

26. _____ energy that produces electricity using the flow of water

27. _____ energy that turns a windmill to pump water or produce electricity

28. _____ energy produced by the heat beneath Earth's surface

29. _____ energy produced from burning organic materials, such as wood

30. _____ fuel produced when plants are changed into alcohol and then mixed with gasoline

FITNESS FLASH: Do 10 jumping jacks.

Find the volume of each solid. Round to the nearest hundredth. Show your work on a separate sheet of paper.

1.

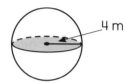

V = _____

2.

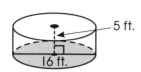

V = _____

3.

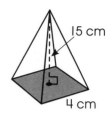

V = _____

4.

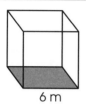

V = _____

5.

V = _____

6.

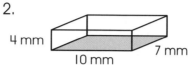

V = _____

Add commas where they are needed in each sentence.

7. When Nathan found a package that was left unattended he immediately notified airport security.

8. The answer of course is yes.

9. In spite of his fear of heights Richard bought a plane ticket to California yesterday.

10. The Union Pacific and Central Pacific Railroads met at Promontory Point Utah on May 10 1869.

11. Mrs. Ancelet our eighth-grade math teacher challenges students to perform to the best of their abilities.

12. While Veterans Day is marked by parades and a holiday from work Americans also should remember the men and women who served and sacrificed for their country.

DAY 15

Read the passage. Then, answer the questions.

Sue Hendrickson

As a child, Sue Hendrickson loved to dig and was always searching for treasures. In the mid-1970s, Hendrickson went hiking with friends to an amber mine. A miner showed Hendrickson a piece of amber with a 23-million-year-old insect trapped inside. This began her lifelong search for **fossils**.

Hendrickson began her career as an archaeologist by digging for bones in the deserts of Peru. She worked with a group of archaeologists who searched for bones of water animals in land that was once under the sea. She helped discover whale, dolphin, and seal bones hundreds of miles from existing water.

In 1990, Hendrickson journeyed to South Dakota with an archaeological team that was digging for dinosaur bones. When the team's truck had a flat tire, the other scientists left to get the tire fixed. But, Hendrickson and her dog stayed behind and went for a walk. She wanted to examine some cliffs that they had not had time to explore.

Hendrickson saw some bones on the ground and looked up. Preserved in the sandstone cliff above her was an enormous dinosaur skeleton! The group immediately began to work on the find. They uncovered the largest, most complete *Tyrannosaurus rex* skeleton ever found. The team named the *T. rex* Sue, after its discoverer.

This was not Sue Hendrickson's only adventure. Two years later, she went with other scientists to explore a Spanish trading ship that sank in 1600. They uncovered huge stone jars, 100 skeletons, and more than 400 gold and silver coins at the shipwreck.

13. Which of the following words best describes Sue Hendrickson?

    A. stern   B. adventurous   C. quiet   D. funny

14. What does the word *fossil* mean?

    A. a trace of an ancient animal or plant preserved in Earth's crust

    B. something metal that rusted

    C. one kind of dinosaur

15. In what year did Hendrickson discover the *T. rex* skeleton? _____

16. How did Hendrickson find the *T. rex* bones?

    A. She was digging in the earth with scientists when they found the skeleton.

    B. Her dog found the bones and ran back to get her.

    C. She went for a walk while she was waiting for a flat tire to be fixed.

> **CHARACTER CHECK:** Draw a comic strip showing a character who demonstrates determination.

A stem-and-leaf plot is one way to organize a set of data. In a stem-and-leaf plot, the greatest place value common to a group of numbers is used for the stem. The lower place values form the leaves. For example, if a set of data contained the numbers 11, 14, 15, and 16, the stem and leaf plot would look like this: 1 | 1, 4, 5, 6.

1. Write two situations in which you might want to use a stem-and-leaf plot to

    organize numbers. _____

    _____

Use the stem-and-leaf plot to answer the questions.

Stem	Leaf
4	6, 8
5	2, 8, 9
6	1, 2, 5, 5
7	3, 4, 4

2. List the numbers in the stem.

    _____

3. How many numbers have stem 6?

    _____

4. Name the low number and the high number.

    _____

5. What is the range?

    _____

Add commas where they are needed in each sentence. Write _A_ if the commas separate an appositive or appositive phrase, _D_ for a direct address, or _P_ for a parenthetical expression.

6. _____ The answer of course is 44.

7. _____ Bridget the tallest girl on the team is a great tennis player.

8. _____ If you wait Justin we will go with you.

9. _____ Button stop scratching the cushions.

10. _____ Nadia please call your brother on the phone.

11. _____ I told you Shay not to wait too long to start your project.

12. _____ Mrs. Ramirez the hardest seventh-grade English teacher gave me an A on my essay.

DAY 16

Read each effect. Then, write a possible cause.

Cause	Effect
13. _____ _____	A. Looking haggard, Melissa arrived late for biology class.
14. _____ _____	B. Thousands of people, some in red and blue caps, others in green and white, gathered in the large arena.
15. _____ _____	C. The Canadian gymnast performed her best balance beam routine to win an Olympic gold medal.
16. _____ _____	D. Crying, Jackie clutched her crimson purse and began the long walk home.
17. _____ _____	E. Dr. Peoples asked the patient to go to the third floor for a chest X-ray.

A physical change occurs with force, such as motion, temperature, or pressure. For example, when energy (heat) is added to ice, it melts. The state of matter has changed, but the chemical composition remains the same. When a chemical change occurs, an object's molecules change. A new substance with a different chemical makeup is formed. For example, when iron rusts, change occurs over a long period of time. Iron molecules combine with oxygen to become iron oxide.

Identify each change as a physical change or a chemical change.

18. water freezing _____

19. wood burning _____

20. frying an egg _____

21. glass breaking _____

22. food spoiling _____

FACTOID: An adult elephant eats an average of 550 pounds (249.5 kg) of vegetation each day.

Use the following information to determine the probability (*P*) of each event occurring. Simplify if possible.

A jar contains 18 jelly beans: 7 purple jelly beans, 3 green jelly beans, and 8 orange jelly beans. Without looking, Travis picks 1 jelly bean from the jar. What is the probability of each of the following outcomes?

1. P(green) = _____

2. P(purple) = _____

3. P(orange) = _____

4. P(not green) = _____

5. P(purple or green) = _____

6. P(not orange) = _____

Read each sentence. Add punctuation as needed.

7. The weather forecaster on Channel 7 said We could have at least two inches of rain tonight.

8. The Celebrated Jumping Frog of Calaveras County is one of Mark Twain's best known short stories.

9. Anita asked her older brother Could I please have a slice of that pizza?

10. No matter how well I prepare for a test said Jason I still get nervous until I can review the test in my hands.

11. What a Wonderful World sung by Louis Armstrong has long been considered a classic.

12. If you practice every day Coach Bradley said you will play better as a team.

DAY 17

Many nonfiction books contain features that convey or organize information in different ways for the reader. Write each book feature from the word bank next to its definition.

table of contents	index	glossary	pictures
title page	caption	bibliography	

13. _____ an alphabetical list of special terms and their definitions found in the back of a book

14. _____ a list of reference books and articles found in the back of the book

15. _____ an alphabetical list at the back of the book that includes people, places, key words, or topics in the book, with page numbers for quick reference

16. _____ a description or explanation for a photograph or illustration

17. _____ a page at the front of the book listing the book title and author, and usually the publisher

18. _____ illustrations or photographs

19. _____ a chronological list of chapters and corresponding page numbers found at the front of the book

Power Walking

Power walking is a great exercise for building endurance. Set a time or distance goal for your first power walk. Then, think of some places where you can walk. Plan to walk with a friend, parent, or guardian in your neighborhood, on a trail at a local park, or at a mall. Set monthly goals to increase your walking time or distance. Track your progress and before you know it, you will be walking miles and improving your endurance and overall fitness!

FITNESS FLASH: Hop on your left foot 10 times.

* See page ii.

Use the information below to determine the probability of each event occurring. Simplify if possible.

A die with sides numbered 1 to 6 is rolled. Find the probability of rolling each outcome.

1. P(5) = _____

2. P(1 or 2) = _____

3. P(odd number) = _____

4. P(not 6) = _____

5. P(even number) = _____

6. P(1, 2, 3, or 4) = _____

Read each sentence. Add semicolons, commas, and colons as needed.

7. Mr. Cole decided to meet with Ms. Grayson Ben's math teacher Mr. Robbins his science teacher and Mrs. Abernathy his English teacher.

8. Raymond Webb just graduated from college he plans to attend law school.

9. The first rule in this class respect other students' rights.

10. The parent company left its main facility open but closed plants in Greensboro North Carolina Jacksonville Florida and Harrisburg Pennsylvania.

11. Will Rogers made this comment on attitude "Don't let yesterday use up too much of today."

12. Alyson accepted the job as a telemarketer for one reason she wanted to work at home while Amy was a baby.

13. Have you ever heard the quote "You can't afford the luxury of a negative thought"?

14. Grace did well in three subjects therefore she will have a high average at the end of the semester.

DAY 18

Read the passage. Then, answer the questions.

The Tang Dynasty

For many years, China was governed by a series of dynasties, or rulers from the same families. The Tang Dynasty, which ruled from about AD 618 to 907, is considered to have been one of the most prosperous dynasties. This period is referred to as China's Golden Age. The arts, including theater, dance, sculpting, and painting, were all valued and very popular during this time. More than one million people lived in the capital city of Chang'an. Farmers were allowed to own land, although this later changed. People who wanted to work in the government had to pass a difficult exam. Only the smartest and most educated people could serve as government officials. The Tang Dynasty charged taxes per individual in a family instead of by property owned. So, the government conducted a very accurate census to determine the empire's population, and households paid taxes on grain and cloth. Trade inside China and to other countries also flourished because new roads and canals built by the previous Sui Dynasty made travel easier. Today, the period ruled by the Tang Dynasty is remembered as a time of great cultural achievement.

15. What is the main idea of this passage?
    A. The Tang government taxed grain and cloth.
    B. The Tang Dynasty lasted for nearly 300 years.
    C. The Tang Dynasty ruled during a period of great cultural achievement.

16. What artistic activities were popular during the Tang Dynasty? _____
    _____

17. How did people become government officials? _____
    _____

18. Why did the government conduct a census? _____
    _____

19. Why did trade during the Tang Dynasty flourish? _____
    _____

FACTOID: One out of every two people in the world is under the age of 25.

Find the mean, median, mode, and range of each data set.

1. 34, 41, 33, 41, 31

    mean: _____

    median: _____

    mode: _____

    range: _____

2. 7, 14, 10, 14, 29, 16, 15

    mean: _____

    median: _____

    mode: _____

    range: _____

3. 18, 10, 10, 8, 35, 10, 21

    mean: _____

    median: _____

    mode: _____

    range: _____

4. 41, 18, 24, 41, 72, 82, 16

    mean: _____

    median: _____

    mode: _____

    range: _____

Read the passage. Add punctuation and correct any other errors as necessary.

The origin of the ice-cream cone has been controversial for several centuries some historians claim that the first paper cone came from France while others maintain that metal cones were used in Germany. Still other people say that an Italian genius introduced the first ice-cream cone.

Ice cream was referred to in Europe as iced pudding and the cones were called wafers. Eating establishments often served the wafers after a meal to soothe digestion. But, once chefs rolled the wafers into funnels the cones could be filled with anything including ice cream.

However many Americans believe that the first edible ice-cream cone was created in the United States. Italo Marchiony who emigrated from Italy created edible cones and sold them from pushcarts in the streets of New York City for a penny each. Marchiony eventually patented his invention in 1903.

DAY 19

Choose the word or the phrase in each group that does not belong. Then, explain your selection.

5. A. central
    B. cirrus
    C. stratus
    D. cumulus

    _____

6. A. pulley
    B. wedge
    C. crate
    D. screw

    _____

7. A. oxygen
    B. hydrogen
    C. helium
    D. calcium

    _____

8. A. skeletal
    B. temperature
    C. muscular
    D. circulatory

    _____

9. A. artery
    B. membrane
    C. ribosome
    D. mitochondrion

    _____

Create a glossary for a book about superheroes. What words might be included in such a glossary? Be creative. Invent new words or special definitions. Create at least 20 entries for your superhero glossary. Use a separate sheet of paper if needed.

_____

_____

_____

_____

FITNESS FLASH: Hop on your right foot for 30 seconds.

* See page ii.

Find the mean, median, mode, and range of each data set.

1. 27, 19, 18, 19, 36

   mean: _____

   median: _____

   mode: _____

   range: _____

2. 12, 16, 32, 11, 12, 17, 19

   mean: _____

   median: _____

   mode: _____

   range: _____

3. 44, 22, 10, 7, 53, 7, 36

   mean: _____

   median: _____

   mode: _____

   range: _____

4. 27, 81, 44, 56, 67, 56, 56

   mean: _____

   median: _____

   mode: _____

   range: _____

Read each pair of sentences. Circle the letter of the sentence that contains an error.

5. A. The dance was a lot of fun.
   B. Me and my friend got home late.

6. A. She did good on the exam.
   B. My dad works many hours.

7. A. Is your bicycle broke?
   B. My ankle looks like it is swollen.

8. A. I don't want no homework.
   B. Did you mean to say that?

9. A. Sam and I walked to the store.
   B. She changed it's tire.

10. A. Trenton spread alot of jam on the bread.
    B. Can you wait a minute?

11. A. The ocean was so choppy.
    B. There car would not start.

12. A. He played bad.
    B. The tennis game had no winner.

DAY 20

Ellen, Julie, Ben, and Dante are athletes. Each person participates in a different sport: tennis, golf, skating, and track. All four athletes are sitting at a square table. Use the information below and deductive reasoning to determine each person's sport and where each athlete is sitting.

- The runner sits across from Dante.
- The tennis player sits on Julie's right.
- Dante and Julie sit next to each other.
- A man sits to the left of the runner.
- The skater sits to the left of the tennis player.

Write the name of each Renaissance figure next to his description.

Miguel de Cervantes	Nicolaus Copernicus
John Milton	Galileo Galilei
Leonardo da Vinci	Johannes Gutenberg
Michelangelo	

13. _____ invented the mechanical printing press.

14. _____ was a novelist, poet, and playwright whose book, *Don Quixote*, is considered to be the first modern novel.

15. _____ was a painter, sculptor, architect, and engineer who sculpted *David* and painted the ceiling of the Sistine Chapel.

16. _____ was a physicist, mathematician, and astronomer known for his belief that the sun was the center of the universe.

17. _____ was a scientist, artist, inventor, and mathematician whose most famous painting is the *Mona Lisa*.

18. _____ was a poet and author of *Paradise Lost*.

19. _____ was the first astronomer to argue that Earth is not the center of the universe.

CHARACTER CHECK: Write five things that you are grateful for.

Erosion

Wind, water, and ice can shape and reshape various landforms on the earth's surface. Over time, sand dunes recede, boulders break into sand, and jagged mountains become gently rolling hills. Erosion is the movement of rock and soil from one area to another area on the earth's surface.

Materials:
- small plastic container
- cup of potting soil
- modeling clay
- measuring teaspoon
- cup of sand
- cup of water
- ice cube

Procedure:
Pour the sand into the plastic container. Gently blow on the sand. What happened? This resembles how wind affects sand. Wind picks up sand from one place and moves it to a different place. This is called wind erosion. Carefully pour the sand back into the cup.

Pour the soil into the plastic container. Firmly pack the soil into the bottom of the container. Carefully pour a small river of water down the middle of the soil. Move the cup in a back-and-forth motion while pouring until the cup is empty. What did the water do to the soil? Over time, water can have the same effect on rock. This is called water erosion. Carefully pour the soil back into the cup.

Press the modeling clay into the bottom of the plastic container. Sprinkle 1 teaspoon (5 mL) of sand on top of the clay. Rub the ice cube over the sand. What happened to the sand? What happened to the clay? As glaciers move slowly over land, they pick up rocks that scrape the land and leave deep scratches. This is called ice erosion.

Complete the following sentences.

1. Blowing _____ can move dirt and sand from one area to

   another.

2. As _____ flows in rivers and other bodies of water, it picks up

   pebbles and sand along the bottom and the sides.

3. The hard _____ of glaciers scrape across the land, picking up dirt

   and boulders along the way.

BONUS

Examining the Effects of Acid Rain

Acid rain is a serious environmental issue. Acid rain can destroy forests, harm wildlife, and erode buildings, monuments, and statues. Acid rain is produced when water vapor in the air reacts with sulfur dioxide and nitrogen oxide, which in turn produces sulfuric acid and nitric acid. These chemicals fall to the earth in the form of precipitation, or acid rain. The chemicals are pollutants that come from burning fossil fuels such as coal and gasoline. In this experiment, students will discover how acid rain affects plants.

Materials:
- 4 index cards
- 4 identical potted plants
- tap water
- bottled water
- vinegar
- orange juice
- measuring cups

Procedure:
Use the index cards to label four identical potted plants as follows: *Plant 1: Tap Water, Plant 2: Bottled Water, Plant 3: Tap Water and Vinegar, Plant 4: Tap Water and Orange Juice.*

Water all of the plants with the same amount of liquid at the same time. Give plant 1 tap water, plant 2 bottled water, and plant 3 a 1:1 mixture of tap water and vinegar. For example, add 1/4 cup (59 mL) of vinegar to 1/4 cup (59 mL) of tap water. Then, give plant 4 a 1:1 mixture of tap water and orange juice.

Place the plants near a window or in a well-lit area so that they receive the same amount of light. How does each plant look? Record your observations in the chart. Then, use what you have learned to complete the conclusion below.

	Week 1	Week 2	Week 3	Week 4
Plant 1				
Plant 2				
Plant 3				
Plant 4				

The _____ and _____ mixtures are similar to acid rain in how they affect plants. _____ contains an acid called citric acid. _____ is an acid too. These two substances mixed with water duplicate the effects of acid rain on the plants. The acids weaken the plants, and when the plants are not given fresh water, they die.

Budgeting

The U.S. federal government receives money from taxes and decides how to spend it. With many costs and programs to fund, it is often difficult to decide how much to spend on each item. The government frequently borrows money to pay for all of these costs and programs. This borrowed money becomes the national debt.

Below is a list of things you might want to buy or do. Each item on the list has a price range. Assume that the more money you spend, the better product or service you will receive. (Consumer note: This is not always true, but for this activity, pretend it is.) You have only $75 to spend, but you want to do as much as you can with it. You do have some extra money in your savings account, and your brother said that he would also lend you some money.

You must decide which items or services you will buy and how much you will spend on each. Try not to borrow from your savings or your brother because you will go into debt. Circle your choices and write what you chose to spend on each. At the bottom of the page, show your total spent. Then, explain why you chose to purchase each item.

_____ gift for Mom ($10–$25)

_____ cell phone ($5–$40)

_____ cell phone service ($25–$38)

_____ video game ($15–$33)

_____ shoes ($29–$50)

_____ scooter ($22–$48)

_____ helmet and pads for scooter ($15–$20)

_____ book ($7–$16)

_____ guitar ($31–$50)

_____ guitar lessons ($5–$9)

_____ pizza ($6–$12)

_____ movie ticket ($2–$8)

Total Spent: _____

Why did you choose to purchase each item? _____

_____

_____

BONUS

Comparing Countries

For the countries below, research and write one fact for each category.

	Argentina	Finland	Cambodia
Population			
Capital City			
Official Language(s)			
Type of Government			
Products			

Abolitionists

Abolitionists were people who spoke out against slavery. In the years leading up to the U.S. Civil War, abolitionists worked to declare slavery against the law. Slave owners did not think anything was wrong with owning slaves. They thought of slaves as property or something they owned. Many abolitionists helped run the Underground Railroad, which helped slaves find safety.

The abolitionists did not have TVs, the Internet, or even radios. So, how did they get people to listen to them? They used newspapers, wrote books, and gave speeches.

Imagine that you are going to give a speech against slavery. Answer the questions to help you plan your speech.

Circle your choices.

1. You are going to pretend to be
    A. an escaped slave.
    B. a writer for a newspaper.
    C. a politician.

2. You are going to write your speech about
    A. the terrible lives of slaves.
    B. your belief that the laws must change.
    C. your own feelings about slavery.

3. You would like the people who hear your speech to mostly feel
    A. angry about slavery.
    B. sad about the slaves in the South.
    C. happy for the slaves who escaped.
    D. sure that they should speak out about the wrongs of slavery.

Finish each sentence as though you are preparing your speech. Then, write your speech on a separate sheet of paper.

4. The main reason I am giving a speech about slavery is _____

_____ .

5. I have spoken about slavery _____ times before.

6. One detail I will use in my speech is _____

_____ .

BONUS

Take It Outside!

With the assistance of a family member, plan a family trip to a special summer event. Discuss the possible costs, such as the cost of fuel, food, entrance, and parking. Make a list of these expenses. Then, project the costs for each item and the total cost for the family trip. On the day of the event, review the budget with your family. Keep all receipts as money is spent. Add all receipts at the end of the day. How much was spent? Did you stay on budget? Did you go over or under budget? Share the results with your family.

Find a place in your community that sells alternative energy sources. Call ahead to schedule a visit. Take a pen and a notebook with you and interview a salesperson regarding the benefits of using the alternative energy source. Ask for brochures that explain the apparatus or the facility's function and purpose. After the interview, review your notes and the brochures. Then, create a 30-second commercial about the benefits of using this alternative energy source. Send a thank-you letter to the person you interviewed.

With an adult, visit an area in your community where people exercise outdoors. With a pen and a notebook, list the various activities that you see people doing, such as running, cycling, walking, or kayaking. Then, tally the number of people doing each activity. At the end of one hour, count the tally marks. Determine how many people you saw exercising and the percentages for each form of exercise observed. Which form of exercise had the highest percentage? Which had the lowest?

Section I

Day 1: 1. 661.01; 2. 215.145; 3. 716.4; 4. 39.653; 5. 19.7; 6. 32.1; 7. 21.5; 8. 64; 9. 96; 10. 33; Students should capitalize the words in green: **American** pioneers followed several routes on their journeys west. Pioneers from **New England** traveled across **New York** on the **Mohawk Trail**. **Another** route led through the **Cumberland Gap**, a natural pass in the **Appalachian Mountains** that ends near the borders of **Kentucky**, **Tennessee**, and **Virginia**.

The first groups of settlers crossing the **Appalachian Mountains** in the late 1700s and early 1800s followed these early trails. The popular **Conestoga** wagon, which originated in **Pennsylvania** and was probably introduced by **Mennonite German** settlers, carried many pioneers migrating southward through the Great **Appalachian Valley** along the Great **Wagon Road**.; 11. D; 12. B; 13. B; 14. D; 15. A; 16. F; 17. E; 18. G; 19. A; 20. C; 21. B; 22. D

Day 2: 1. 494.832; 2. 6.38; 3. 95.75; 4. 104.53; 5. 23.376; 6. 310.42; 7. 2.44; 8. 120.68; 9. 95.46; 10. 6.82; 11. the team member's athletic shoes; 12. Mom's breakfast; 13. the students' rights; 14. Oakland's weather; 15. The architect's plans; 16. the crowd's enthusiasm; 17. N; 18. P; 19. N; 20. N; 21. P; 22. P; 23. P; 24. P; 25. C; 26. firsthand information about an event from the view of someone who was present when the event happened; 27. information from primary sources; 28. Answers will vary.

Day 3: 1. 12; 2. 14.43; 3. 21.58; 4. 2.19; 5. 15.44; 6. 91.26; 7. 1.35; 8. 57.2; 9. 9.85; 10. 1.86; 11. A; 12. I; 13. C; 14. G; 15. E; 16. B; 17. H; 18. J; 19. K; 20. D; 21. F; 22. B; 23. B; 24. A

Day 4: 1. =; 2. <; 3. <; 4. >; 5. <; 6. <; 7. <; 8. =; 9. >; 10. $\frac{4}{12}$, $\frac{6}{12}$, $\frac{9}{12}$; $\frac{1}{3}$, $\frac{1}{2}$, $\frac{3}{4}$; 11. $\frac{4}{18}$, $\frac{6}{18}$, $\frac{15}{18}$, $\frac{2}{9}$; $\frac{1}{3}$, $\frac{5}{6}$; 12. $\frac{4}{24}$, $\frac{18}{24}$, $\frac{21}{24}$, $\frac{1}{6}$, $\frac{3}{4}$, $\frac{7}{8}$;

13. A; 14. A; 15. C; 16. A; 17. C; 18. bulldozer; 19. doze; 20. perilous; 21. recipe; 22. breakfast; 23. charcoal

Day 5: 1. $\frac{37}{35}$; 2. $\frac{1}{9}$; 3. $\frac{35}{36}$; 4. $\frac{41}{24}$; 5. $\frac{17}{18}$; 6. $\frac{3}{50}$; 7. $\frac{1}{24}$; 8. $\frac{49}{8}$; 9. $\frac{1}{40}$; 10. $\frac{11}{12}$; 11. $\frac{11}{20}$; 12. $\frac{5}{4}$;

13–18. Students should circle the words in green: 13. **knowing**, know; 14. **hearing**, hear; 15. **floating**, float; 16. **complaining**, complain; 17. **putting**, putt; 18. **going**, go; 19. A; 20. B; 21. B; 22. B; 23. A; 24. A

Day 6: 1. $\frac{1}{40}$; 2. $\frac{1}{28}$; 3. $\frac{1}{96}$; 4. $\frac{12}{35}$; 5. $\frac{3}{5}$; 6. $\frac{8}{21}$; 7. $\frac{35}{24}$; 8. $\frac{27}{2}$; 9. $\frac{20}{3}$; 10. $\frac{35}{4}$; 11. $\frac{14}{9}$; 12. $\frac{1}{2}$; 13–19. Students should underline the words in green twice: 13. **is**, novel → The Book Thief; 14. **is**, author → Charles Dickens; 15. **is**, wizard → One; 16. **is**, tale → story; 17. **is**, book → Harry Potter and the Sorcerer's Stone; 18. **is**, book → The Westing Game; 19. **are**, novels → Animal Farm and 1984; 20. They wanted each state to have the same number of representatives so that less-populated states would have as much say as more-populated states; 21. They would have more votes than the smaller states; 22. when two sides make concessions to reach an agreement; 23–24. Answers will vary.

Day 7: 1. $8\frac{1}{6}$; 2. $13\frac{5}{12}$; 3. $9\frac{5}{8}$; 4. $19\frac{5}{24}$; 5. $61\frac{4}{5}$; 6. $24\frac{8}{9}$; 7. $1\frac{13}{16}$; 8. $3\frac{5}{7}$; 9. $5\frac{11}{15}$; 10. outlet; 11. gift; 12. bracelet; 13. minutes; 14. life; 15. roses; 16. Miss Osbourne; 17. career; 18. B; 19. A; 20. C; 21. C; 22. A; 23. B; Nick: jersey number 20, 10 minutes; Joey: jersey number 13, 11 minutes; Beki: jersey number 34, 12 minutes; Carmen: jersey number 2, 14 minutes

Day 8: 1. $2\frac{2}{7}$; 2. $14\frac{1}{4}$; 3. 18; 4. 54; 5. $1\frac{1}{3}$; 6. $13\frac{17}{20}$; 7. $3\frac{13}{42}$; 8. $5\frac{1}{14}$; 9. $12\frac{19}{40}$; 10. class; 11. them; 12. you; 13. me; 14. us; 15. him; 16. her; 17. Miss Sherman; 18. volunteers;

19. brother; 20–27. Answers will vary but may include: 20. drew a line in the sand, created a boundary; 21. keep your shirt on, stay calm; 22. went belly up, died; 23. keep a straight face, not show emotion; 24. in a dead heat, in a tie; 25. a bull in a china shop, clumsily breaking things; 26. wade through the stack, sort through; 27. jockeyed for position, tried to be first in line

Day 9: 1. 0.8; 2. 0.375; 3. 0.6; 4. 0.6; 5. 0.85; 6. 0.04; 7. 0.225; 8. 0.72; 9. 75%; 10. 25%; 11. 50%; 12. 10%; 13. 11%; 14. 73%; 15. 20%; 16. 5%; 17–22. Students should circle the words in green: 17. Wendy, **necklace**; 18. her, **dinner**; 19. him, **recognition**; 20. brother, **DVD**; 21. Juana, **grip**; 22. explorers, **trouble**; 23. A; 24. A; 25. A

Day 10: 1. 38%; 2. 1,080%; 3. 1,239%; 4. 52,332%; 5. 238%; 6. 63%; 7. 11%; 8. 48%; 9. 31%; 10. 232%; 11. 1,745%; 12. 529%; 13. Anna, a great actress, got the lead role in the play.; 14. The United Nations, an influential international organization, is based in New York City.; 15. Bridget and Connor, both geologists, work at the Field Museum in Chicago, Illinois.; 16–22. Students should circle the words in green: 16. S, **Roger, eagle**; 17. M, **uncle, treasure**; 18. M, **flying papers and ringing phones, blizzard**; 19. S, **clown, goose**; 20. S, **Perry, cheetah**; 21. S, **he, ox**; 22. M, **life, dream**

Day 11: 1. 3; 2. 28.57; 3. 123.08; 4. 18; 5. 16.67; 6. 375; 7. 11.25; 8. 50.77; 9. 333.33; 10. 24.05; 11. 44.44; 12. 154.55; 13. 17.6; 14. 633.33; 15. 104; 16. I, everyone; 17. P, You; 18. P, He; 19. P, them; 20. P, It; 21. P, you; 22. I, Neither; 23. P, They; 24. D, These; 25. P, I; 26. D, That; 27. I, Many; 28. D, This; 29. I, anybody; 30. Internet; 31. atlas; 32. almanac; 33. newspaper or magazine; 34. encyclopedia; 35. nonfiction books; 36. B; 37. F; 38. H; 39. J; 40. A; 41. D; 42. E; 43. G; 44. C; 45. I

Day 12: 1. $24.70; 2. 33%; 3. $1.54; 4. $23,655.91; 5. R; 6. I; 7. I; 8. R; 9. R; 10. I; 11. R; 12. I; 13. R; 14. R; 15. F; 16. T; 17. T; 18. F; 19. T; 20. F; 21. F

Day 13: 1. 60; 2. 36; 3. ⁻9; 4. 74; 5. ⁻36; 6. $\frac{1}{3}$; 7–20. Answers will vary; 21. C; 22. C; 23. the ballroom at night.

Day 14: 1. 0; 2. 39; 3. 472; 4. 22; 5. ⁻91; 6. ⁻143; 7. ⁻23; 8. ⁻7; 9. 53; 10. ⁻17; 11. ⁻13; 12. 5; 13. 13; 14. 15; 15. 9; 16–25. Students should circle the words in green: 16. N, **we**; 17. N, **She**; 18. O, **him**; 19. N, **They**; 20. O, **me**; 21. O, **her**; 22. N, **They**; 23. O, **him**; 24. O, **them**; 25. O, **me**; 26. amphibians and reptiles; 27. Answers will vary.

Day 15: 1. 25; 2. ⁻2; 3. 120; 4. ⁻289; 5. 102; 6. 93; 7. ⁻666; 8. 54; 9. ⁻15; 10. ⁻$\frac{35}{6}$; 11. ⁻106; 12. 52; 13. ⁻4; 14. ⁻40; 15. ⁻20; 16. ⁻$\frac{29}{8}$; Stepping off the plane, Mrs. Jackson arrived in Costa Rica at noon. As soon as **she** got to her hotel, **she** enjoyed a light lunch at the restaurant. After lunch, Mr. Jackson, who had taken a different flight, joined **her**. "Let's go to the beach," **he** said. **They** changed into swimsuits, and off **they** went. That evening, **they** called **their** son, Max. "**We** are having a great time," **they** told **him**; 17. drama; 18. fable; 19. folklore; 20. legend; 21. horror; 22. legend

Day 16: 1. 6; 2. 6; 3. 7; 4. 5; 5. 6; 6. 2; 7. A; 8. A, L; 9. A; 10. A, A; 11. L; 12. A, A; 13. A, A; 14. L; 15. L; 16. A, A; 17. B; 18. igneous, sedimentary, metamorphic; 19. Volcanic rock releases magma, which then cools; 20. Water deposits sediment, which compresses into layers over time; 21. They begin as igneous or sedimentary rocks. Then, they are squeezed within Earth's crust.

Day 17: 1. 3⁶; 2. a²b³; 3. 9²; 4. x³y; 5. 10⁵; 6. 4⁵ 5⁴; 7. $\frac{1}{2}$; 8. 14d + 5; 9. ⁻5a; 10–19. Students should underline the words in green twice: 10. **has** attained; 11. **were** used; 12. **had** earned, **were** lost; 13. **would** work; 14. **are** known; 15. **were** painted; 16. **have been** known; 17. **have** called; 18. **was** founded; 19. **can** weigh; 20. mystery; 21. myth; 22. poetry; 23. biography;

24. essay; 25. goods; 26. services; 27. demand; 28. natural resources; 29. inflation; 30. capital resources; 31. supply; 32. scarcity

Day 18: 1. 12; 2. ⁻10; 3. 0; 4. 25; 5. 9; 6. ⁻15; 7. L; 8. AUX; 9. ACT; 10. L; 11. ACT; 12. L; 13. ACT; 14. L; 15. L; 16. AUX; 17. ACT; 18. AUX; 19. ACT; 20. AUX; 21. A; 22. J; 23. D; 24. G; 25. B; 26. H; 27. F; 28. I; 29. C; 30. E; 31. cilia; 32. macronucleus; 33. food vacuole; 34. cytoplasm; 35. anal pore; 36. oral groove; 37. micronucleus; 38. cell membrane

Day 19: 1. positive; 2. negative; 3. negative; 4. positive; 5. positive; 6. negative; 7. ⁻8.1; 8. ⁻30.4 or ⁻30$\frac{2}{5}$; 9. $\frac{20}{21}$; 10. $\frac{18}{25}$; 11. ⁻3.564; 12. $\frac{4}{3}$; 13. forgot, forgotten; 14. taught, taught; 15. sank, sunk; 16. broke, broken; 17. froze, frozen; 18. threw, thrown; 19. chose, chosen; 20. heard, heard; 21. woke, woken; 22. ate, eaten; 23. rode, ridden; 24. C; 25. C; 26. C

Day 20: 1. 7c, 12c; 2. none; 3. 5t, 7t; 4. none; 5. 5r, ⁻10r; 6. q, 2q, 5q; 7. 5m; 8. already simplified; 9. 2a; 10. 23y; 11. 18q + 14; 12. 5t + 4m; 13–22. Students should circle the words in green: 13. PAST, **enjoyed**; 14. PAST, **did not hear**; 15. FUT, **will teach**; 16. PAST, **ate**; 17. PAST, **gave**; 18. PRE, **migrate**; 19. PRE, **enjoys**; 20. PAST, **burned**; 21. PAST, **glanced**; 22. FUT, **will announce**; Answers will vary but may include: the perfect pet for everyone, fantastic addition to every home, all turtles are lazy, dogs or cats are cute and frisky, turtles are sluggish but still fascinating, you will have to purchase

Bird Adaptations: Answers will vary.

Using Latitude and Longitude:
1. Hong Kong; 2. London; 3. Atlanta; 4. Edinburgh; 5. New Delhi; 6. Johannesburg; 7. Barcelona; 8. Calgary; 9. San Francisco; 10. São Paulo; 11. 49°N, 2°E; 12. 49°N, 123°W; 13. 40°N, 116°E; 14. 38°N, 24°E; 15. 12°S, 77°W; 16. 42°N, 71°W; 17. 21°N, 158°W; 18. 19°N, 99°W; 19. 45°N, 12°E; 20. 56°N, 37°E

Forms of Government: Answers will vary.

The Panama Canal: Design and items on timelines will vary.

Section II

Day 1: 1. ⁻5; 2. 28y; 3. ⁻18x + 15y − 12xy; 4. 9x + 21y; 5. x + 5y + 5; 6. 3x² − 2y² + 6x + 9xy²; 7. ⁻7x + 20y; 8. ⁻6c + 4d; 9. ⁻4a − 26b; 10. ⁻x − 2y; 11. 25x + 90y; 12. 18x − 12y; 13. 27x − 9y; 14. ⁻6a − 16b + 24z; 15. ⁻23x; 16. ⁻6y² + 3y − 6x − 9; 17. had finished; 18. had driven; 19. had sung; 20. have visited; 21. have bought; 22. has read; 23. will have finished; 24. N; 25. P; 26. P; 27. P; 28. P; 29. N; 30. N; 31. N; 32. translucent; 33. opaque; 34. diffuse reflection; 35. ray; 36. reflection; 37. convex; 38. lens; 39. transparent; 40. focal point; 41. concave

Day 2: 1. x = 8; 2. a = 45; 3. z = 56; 4. x = 5; 5. a = 2; 6. b = 3; 7. t = 42; 8. y = 5; 9. m = 3; 10. z = 10; 11. t = 48; 12. x = 9; 13–22. Students should circle the words in orange: 13. present progressive, **is running**; 14. past progressive, **was staying**; 15. past perfect; **had told**; 16. future progressive, **will be approving**; 17. present perfect, **have played**; 18. past progressive, **were swaying**; 19. future progressive, **will be interviewing**; 20. A; 21. a network of trade routes leading from Asia to the West; 22. goods such as gold, silver, silk, and spices; 23. It was several thousand miles long and was considered dangerous; 24. the magnetic compass

Day 3: 1. x = 33; 2. t = 9; 3. m = ⁻17; 4. k = 0; 5. s = ⁻7; 6. r = ⁻14; 7. d = ⁻7; 8. h = ⁻7; 9. c = ⁻1; 10. j = ⁻19; 11. p = 0; 12. z = 3; 13. has decided; 14. had closed; 15. will have seen; 16. will have played; 17. have cut; 18. A; 19. B; 20. A; 21. A; 22. B; 23. A; 24. Answers will vary but may include: work with children or the elderly; clean parks; hold road races; sell baked goods; hold yard sales; provide for people in need of food, shelter, or clothing

Day 4: 1. y + 6 = 12; 2. 56 = 7 • t; 3. 17 + a = 21; 4. k + 11 = 32; 5. 4 + x = 12;

6. 3 = 8 + *r*; 7. 15 • *h* = 75; 8. 39 = *f* • 13; 9–18. Students should circle the words in orange: 9. <u>beads</u>, **are**; 10. **is**, <u>gate</u>; 11. <u>Tucson</u>, **lies**; 12. <u>Hawks, Eagles, and Cardinals</u>, **are**; 13. <u>tower</u>, **is**; 14–18. Answers will vary; 19. Root Word: beauty, Suffix: -ful; 20. Root Word: kind, Suffix: -ness; 21. Root Word: friend, Suffix: -ly; 22. Root Word: cheer, Suffix: -ful; 23. Prefix: in-, Root Word: complete; 24. Root Word: tree, Suffix: -less; 25. Prefix: in-, Root Word: definite, Suffix: -ly

Day 5: 1. (8 + 2) + 17, 27; 2. 3 • (25 • 4), 300; 3. (75 + 25) + 19, 119; 4. 3 • (⁻4 • 250), ⁻3,000; 5. 21 + (45 + 55), 121; 6. (⁻20 • 50) • ⁻29, 29,000; 7. (68 + 32) + 54, 154; 8. 12 • (5 • 20), 1,200; 9. (5 • 10) • 18, 900; 10–17. Students should circle the words in orange: 10. <u>Gretchen</u>, **goes**; 11. <u>Carlos, Ben</u>, **have been**; 12. <u>statue</u>, **stands**; 13. <u>teams</u>, **call**; 14. <u>Trail Ridge Road</u>, **winds**; 15. <u>questions</u>, **were**; 16. <u>president</u>, <u>vice president</u>, **run**; 17. <u>Kiley Smith</u>, **brings**; 18. A; 19. C; 20. 3, 4, 2, 1; 21. He made it possible for people of all races to participate in sports.

Day 6: 1. 3; 2. *t*; 3. 4(12) + 4(15); 4. 3(*a* + 2*b*); 5. 10*t* + 13*t*; 6. 6*x* + 8*x*; 7. *r*(7 + 8) + 2; 8. 2(5*x*) + 2(8*y*) or 10*x* + 16*y*; 9. 8*a* + 15; 10. 4*k* + 12; 11. 10*b* + 8; 12. 17*c* + 27; 13–17. Answers will vary but may include: 13. The movie, *The Sound of Music*, fascinated me.; 14. The deputy's words amazed the young children in the classroom.; 15. Meghan's cat, Buffy, chased the toy.; 16. When Lucy opened the soft drink, it sprayed her in the face.; 17. Andy Rahal scored a goal for the Crosby Middle School soccer team.; 18. C; 19. B; 20. B; 21. A; 22. D; 23. D; 24. C; 25. A

Day 7: 1. *x* = 2; 2. *d* = 7$\frac{1}{2}$; 3. *l* = 16; 4. *m* = 33$\frac{1}{3}$; 5. *n* = 1; 6. *t* = 9; 7. *v* = 1.4; 8. *z* = 3$\frac{1}{5}$; 9. *s* = 36; 10. *c* = 24; 11. *r* = 3; 12. *b* = 18; 13. *k* = 3; 14. *w* = 4; 15. *f* = 4; 16. *h* = 16$\frac{2}{3}$; 17. Four million, L; this, L; beautiful, D; majestic, D; 18. long, D; interesting, D; detailed, D; human,

D; 19. Three, L; lost, D; two, L; park, D; 20. smaller, D; this, L; 21. taller, D; heavier, D; 22. bright, D; cheerful, D; 23–29. Students should circle the words in orange: 23. S, **Detective Oakley, fox**; 24. S, **I, lark**; 25. S, **love, steel**; 26. S, **Louise, fish**; 27. S, **hand, ice**; 28. M, **grandson, sunshine**; 29. M, **Ralph, mule**; 30. key, ring; 31. ring, finger; 32. finger, snap; 33. snap, dragon; 34. dragon, fly; 35. fly, ball; 36. ball, game

Day 8: 1. $8.75; 2. 18 ounces; 3. $12.50; 4. $1.76; 5. $9.15; 6. $42.88; 7. sympathetic; 8. most honest; 9. more active; 10. monstrous; 11. more ominous; 12. youngest; 13. most famous; 14. They support a dazzling array of life; 15. B; 16. C; 17. to form limestone to support their soft bodies

Day 9: 1. 50%; 2. 19%; 3. 45; 4. 20; 5. 15.32; 6. 84; 7. 25%; 8. 90; 9. 38.88; 10. 58%; 11. A; 12. P; 13. A; 14. P; 15. P; 16. P; 17. A; 18. P; 19. P; 20. P; 21. B; 22. D; 23. F; 24. A; 25. G; 26. E; 27. C; 28. H

Day 10:

1–8. Students should circle the words in orange: 1. **vastly** → different; 2. **exceptionally** → talented; 3. **bravely** → donned, **outside** → stepped; 4. **uniquely** → dressed; 5. **really** → wonderful; 6. **professionally** → arranged; 7. **quietly** → tiptoe; 8. **truly** → happy; 9. C; 10. F; 11. A; 12. H; 13. D; 14. E; 15. B; 16. G; 17. outer core; 18. crust; 19. mantle; 20. lithosphere; 21. inner core; 22. atmosphere

Day 11: 1. right 3, down 2; 2. left 1, up 4; 3. right 7, up 6; 4. left 4, down 5; 5. down 3; 6. right 7; 7. (2,3); 8. (1,⁻5); 9. (⁻6,2); 10. (⁻5,⁻3); 11. (⁻3,6); 12.

(4,⁻2); 13. less costly; 14. beautifully; 15. badly; 16. slowest; 17. more thoroughly; 18. more closely; 19. B; 20. T, F, F, F

Day 12: 1. G; 2. H; 3. C; 4. E; 5. D; 6. J; 7. I; 8. L; 9. B; 10. F; 11. K; 12. A; 13. ADV; 14. ADJ; 15. ADJ; 16. ADV; 17. ADV; 18. ADV; 19. ADV; 20. Answers will vary but may include: Getting sufficient sleep is essential to repair the body and fight sickness; 21. Answers will vary.

Day 13: 1. $\overrightarrow{XY}$; 2. $\overline{DE}$ or $\overline{ED}$; 3. Point S; 4. $\overleftrightarrow{WX}$ or $\overleftrightarrow{XW}$; 5. $\overleftrightarrow{CD}$ or $\overleftrightarrow{DC}$; 6. $\overrightarrow{LM}$; 7. $\overleftrightarrow{JK}$ or $\overleftrightarrow{KJ}$; 8. Point M; 9. $\overrightarrow{HI}$; 10–19. Answers will vary but may include: 10. of, at; 11. in; 12. with; 13. near; 14. from; 15. of; 16. over, on; 17. in; 18. over, by; 19. of; Answers will vary.

Day 14: 1. straight; 2. obtuse; 3. acute; 4. obtuse; 5. right; 6. acute; 7. acute; 8. obtuse; 9. right; 10. acute; 11. obtuse; 12. straight; 13–15. Check student's work.; 16–24. Students should circle the words in orange: 16. **by** the phone, **in** the Louisville, Kentucky, airport; 17. **with** the city; 18. **without** that information; 19. **in** the tree; 20. **to** the movies; 21. **to** the booth, **of** the new broadcast team; 22. **under** the cushions, **of** the sofa; 23. **under** the two buildings; 24. **at** Italian restaurants; 25. B; 26. beautiful mountains, glaciers, Lake Louise, wildlife; 27. Animals reproduce rapidly; It is hard to control misuse; Animals are targets for poachers; 28. geysers, hot springs, scenery; 29. C

Day 15: 1. CAT, 25°; 2. SIJ, 170°; 3. LAM, 90°; 4. XYZ, 125°; 5–14. Conjunctions will vary but may include: 5. or; 6. and; 7. but; 8. but; 9. and; 10. but; 11. and; 12. but; 13. and; 14. and; 15. B; 16. E; 17. I; 18. A; 19. H; 20. C; 21. D; 22. F; 23. G; 24. granite; 25. limestone; 26. slate; 27. marble

Day 16: 1. 90°, complementary; 2. A, supplementary; 3. 45°, 135°, 45°; 4. 180°; 5. 90°; 6. complementary; 7–10. Answers will vary; Mrs. Jackson was unable to buy a new watch; Answers will vary but may include: "You only have $25 in your account"; 11. B; 12. F; 13. B; 14. A; 15. F; 16. D; 17. A; 18. C; 19. E; 20. E.

Day 17: 1. ∠S and ∠Z, ∠T and ∠Y; 2. ∠V and ∠W, ∠U and ∠X; 3. ∠V and ∠X, ∠U and ∠W; 4. ∠T and ∠X, ∠V and ∠Z, ∠S and ∠W, ∠U and ∠Y; 5. corresponding; 6. alternate exterior; 7. alternate interior; 8. consecutive interior; 9. alternate exterior; 10. corresponding; 11–18. Answers will vary but may include: 11. both, and; 12. both, and; 13. either, or; 14. Neither, nor; 15. Both, and; 16. whether, or; 17. both, and; 18. Either, or; 19. C; 20. 3, 2, 5, 1, 4; 21. C

Day 18: 1. triangle, 3; 2. quadrilateral (parallelogram), 4; 3. heptagon, 7; 4. pentagon, 5; 5. nonagon, 9; 6. hexagon, 6; 7. decagon, 10; 8. octagon, 8; 9–14. Answers will vary; 15. T; 16. T; 17. T; 18. P; 19. T; 20. T; 21. T; 22. T; 23. P; 24. P; 25. T; 26. P; 27. P; 28. P; 29–30. Answers will vary; 31. gravity; 32. speed; 33. velocity; 34. weight; 35. friction; 36. force; 37. momentum; 38. inertia; 39. acceleration; 40. mass

Day 19: 1. acute, equilateral; 2. right, scalene; 3. obtuse, scalene; 4. acute, equilateral; 5. acute, scalene; 6. acute, equilateral; 7. right, isosceles; 8. acute, isosceles; 9. right, scalene; 10. V; 11. ADJ; 12. N; 13. N; 14. PREP; 15. CON; 16. PRO; 17. ADV; 18. ADJ; 19. INT; 20. PREP; 21. D; 22. D; 23. C; 24. D; 25. C; 26. A

Day 20: 1. scalene; 2. acute; 3. obtuse; 4. isosceles; 5. right; 6. Marsha; 7. Relatives; 8. Sarah Bernhardt; 9. Jimmy Taylor; 10. Dogs; 11. number; 12. James Buchanan; 13. city; 14. members; 15. shark; 16–21. Answers will vary but may include: 16. Indian and South Pacific Oceans; 17. It has two rows of 80 to 100 tentacles that surround its head; It has an external shell with many chambers; 18. shrimp, fish, molted shell chambers; 19. They attach to rocks, coral, or the sea floor; 20. has arms; 21. cannot change color or squirt ink

Convection Currents: Answers will vary.

Latitude and Longitude: United States and Canada: 1. California; 2. Alberta; 3. the Atlantic Ocean; 4. Georgia; 5. New Mexico; 6. the Arctic Ocean; 7. the Sierra Nevada Mountains; 8. 40°N; 9. 60°N; 10. 40°N, 90°W; 11. 90°W

The Role of Government: 1. E; 2. G; 3. B; 4. I; 5. C; 6. F; 7. D; 8. H; 9. A

International Services: Answers will vary.

If Landmarks Could Talk: 1. Grand Canyon; 2. Taj Mahal; 3. Parthenon; 4. Easter Island; 5. Great Wall of China; 6. Sydney Opera House; 7. Leaning Tower of Pisa; 8. Stonehenge; 9. Sphinx; 10. Mount Rushmore

Section III

Day 1: 78°; 2. 5 mm; 3. 60°; 4. 67; 5. 70°; 6. 61°; 7–14. Circled answers include: 7. Swimming, fishing, hiking, and horseback riding; 8. Iced tea, iced coffee, lemonade, and cold soft drinks; 9. Cindy, Stephanie, and Jeanine; 10. Grover and Linda Flowers; 11. Firefighters and police officers; 12. Tents, sleeping bags, cooking utensils, and other camping gear; 13. Orange roughy, halibut, and swordfish; 14. Benji, Eric, and Winston; 15. Prefix: ex-, Root Word: press, Suffix: -ible; 16. Prefix: un-, Root Word: believe, Suffix: -able; 17. Root Word: drama, Suffix: -tize; 18. Root Word: allow, Suffix: -ance; 19. Prefix: re-, Root Word: search, Suffix: -er; 20. B. 139.20 rubles, 104.20 rubles, $0.83; C. 148.73 yen, $3.00; D. $1.63, $3.37

Day 2: 1. c = 13 m; 2. c = 12.04 cm; 3. c = 7.07 yd.; 4. b = 4.90 ft.; 5. b = 5.20 mm; 6. a = 8 in.; 7. b = 2.24 ft.; 8. a = 3 cm; 9. walked, smiled; 10. knows, can turn; 11. sprinted, slid; 12. ordered, decided; 13. passed, ran; 14. stayed, cleaned; 15. liked, enjoyed; 16. studied, recorded; 17. pounded, roared; 18. bought, built; 19. birdied, bogeyed; 20. paid, withheld; 21. D; 22. C; 23. C; 24. D; 25. A; 26. B

Day 3: 1. 7.5 cm; 2. 3 yd.; 3. 6.5 ft.; 4. 1 m; 5. 52 m; 6. 124 ft.; 7. 72 yd.; 8. 128 mm; 9. S; 10. S; 11. C; 12. S; 13. C; 14. C; 15. S; 16. C; 17. S; 18. C; 19. C; 20. B; 21. Answers will vary; 22. a smaller representative group; 23. by asking a subsample the question

Day 4: 1. A = 24 cm², P = 20 cm; 2. A = 144 in.², P = 48 in.; 3. A = 36 ft.², P = 30 ft.; 4. A = 16 yd.², P = 20 yd.; 5. A = 70 mm², P = 38 mm; 6. A = 64² m, P = 32 m; 7. A = 16 in.², P= 16 in.; 8. A = 72 ft²., P = 36 ft.; 9. A = 21 cm², P = 20 cm; 10. D; 11. I; 12. I; 13. D; 14–17. Students should circle the words in blue: 14. **I want to be the first to volunteer** whenever the teacher asks for help; 15. If you stay until the birthday party is over, **call Mom for a ride home**; 16. When monsoon season begins, **the humidity makes the air uncomfortable**; 17. **Pizza is Crawford's choice for dinner,** but only if it has a thin crust; 18. H; 19. A; 20. I; 21. G; 22. D; 23. E; 24. F; 25. B; 26. C

Day 5: 1. A = 64 m², P = 32 m; 2. A = 70 mm², P = 38 mm; 3. A = 24 yd.², P = 24 yd.; 4. A = 120 m², P = 52 m; 5. A = 100 yd.², P = 64 yd.; 6. A = 52 m², P = 36 m; 7. A = 84 cm², P = 42 cm; 8. A = 354 yd.², P = 76 yd.; 9–13. Students should circle the words in blue: 9. We stopped playing and sought shelter **when the storm began**; 10. Gabe hopped off his skateboard **so that his friend could use it**; 11. We won the state championship **because we played together as a team**; 12. **Although the price of gasoline rose by 50 cents per gallon,** Americans did not curtail their travel plans; 13. **If we fail to finish our project tonight,** we will not be in Mrs. Hooper's good graces tomorrow; 14–21. Rephrased answers will vary but circled words include: 14. off the hook; 15. don't get it; 16. props; 17. What's up?; 18. in; 19. chill; 20. hit it out of the park; 21. C; 22. B; 23. E; 24. F; 25. G; 26. A; 27. D

Day 6: 1. A = 6 yd.², P = 12 yd.; 2. A = 35 m², P = 34 m; 3. 45 in.², P = 34 in.; 4. A = 73.5 ft.², P = 46 ft.; 5. A = 67.5 cm², P = 45 cm; 6. A = 150 yd.², P = 55 yd.; 7. A = 21 m², P = 27 m;

8. A = 54 cm², P = 36 cm; 9. A = 67.5 ft.², P = 39 ft.; 10. F; 11. F; 12. C; 13. F; 14. F; 15. C; 16. C; 17. Answers will vary; 18. D; 19. C; 20. A; 21. C

Day 7: 1. 496 ft.²; 2. 346 mm²; 3. 880 in.²; 4. 188 cm²; 5. 592 m²; 6. 424 yd.²; 7–10. Answers will vary but may include: 7. Colin's dad is the CEO and the president of First Federal Bank.; 8. Our cat, Coz, jumped from the patio to the wall, but he was afraid to jump down the other side into an unfamiliar place.; 9. Lisa lives an active life and is the busiest person I've ever met.; 10. Mrs. Crawford's explanation didn't make sense to Ellie, so she solved the math problem her own way.; Answers will vary but may include: John has been accepted to the college of his choice; 11. E; 12. F; 13. G; 14. D; 15. B; 16. H; 17. C; 18. A

Day 8: 1. 150.80 cm³; 2. 512 ft.³; 3. 2309.07 m³; 4. 300 yd.³; 5. 904.32 in.³; 6. 83.33 mm³; 7–9. Answers will vary but may include: 7. Kelly worked for years as a consultant for Harnquist and Beckman and now has her own consulting firm.; 8. Lake Powell, which occupies parts of both Arizona and Utah, is the largest lake in either state.; 9. We had box seats in the front row, so we could put our drinks on top of the Cardinal 's dugout.; 10. except; 11. immigrated; 12. it's; 13. fare; 14. then; 15. Their; 16. Whose; 17. two; 18. principal; 19. past; 20. that

Day 9: 1. ∠VUT; ∠UVT; ∠UTV; 2. ∠EDC, ∠FJI; ∠ABC, ∠GHI; ∠BAE, ∠HGF; ∠DEA, ∠JFG; ∠DCB, ∠JIH; 3. ∠EFG; ∠FGH; ∠GHE; ∠HEF; 4. ∠NML, ∠SRQ; ∠JNM, ∠OSR; ∠JKL, ∠OPQ; ∠KLM, ∠PQR; ∠NJK, ∠SOP; 5. ∠MNL, ∠PRQ; ∠MLN, ∠PQR; ∠LMN, ∠QPR; 6. ∠ZWX, ∠BCD; ∠XYZ, ∠DAB; ∠WXY, ∠CDA; ∠YZW, ∠ABC; 7. then; 8. which; 9. Your; 10. that; 11. you're; 12. Answers will vary but may include: describing life and landscapes; fields, brook, autumn eve, trees, moon; 13. They enjoy doing it; 14. moon

Day 10:

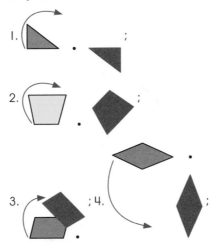

5–8. Answers will vary but may include: 5. Kelly doesn't want any more interruptions.; 6. Kim Tracie never did anything wrong until she broke her mother's favorite vase.; 7. Dr. Canberra was born in Argentina, but he never traveled anywhere else once he arrived in the United States.; 8. I left home without my umbrella since there is not a chance of rain today.; 9. F; 10. T; 11. T; 12. T; 13. F; 14. F; 15. T; 16. Answers will vary; 17. ductile; 18. malleable; 19. alloy; 20. reactivity; 21. conductor; 22. magnetic

Day 11: 1. yes, reduced; 2. yes, reduced; 3. no, not reduced on equal scale; 4. yes, reduced; 5. no, rotated; 6. yes, enlarged; 7. yes, reduced; 8. no, rotated; 9–15. Students should draw three lines under the first letter of the words: 9. Who, Haste; 10. We, American, Indian, Arizona; 11. Tacos, Lindsey's, Mexican; 12. There, Sequoia, National, Park; 13. The, Sunday, May, Mother's, Day, United, States; 14. If; 15. Our, Roosevelt, Middle, School, Wednesday, Labor, Day; B; Underlined details will vary; 16. C; 17. president and cabinet of advisors; 18. House of Representatives and Senate

Day 12: 1. reduction; 2. enlargement; 3. reduction; 4. reduction; 5. enlargement; 6. reduction; 7. enlargement; 8. enlargement; 9. 3:4; 10. 1:3; 11. 3:2; 12. 2:1; 13–19. Students should draw

three lines under the first letter of the words: 13. Col., Carlson, American; 14. Beauty, Beast; 15. I, Sunday; 16. Mom, Dad, Williamsburg, Virginia; 17. Eleanor, Roosevelt, No; 18. The, North, South, Civil, War; 19. The, Secretary, General, United, Nations; 20. B; 21. A; 22. 9 miles (15 km); 23. B; 24. the gravitational pull of the planets

Day 13: 1. 10,560; 2. 15; 3. 12; 4. 5; 5. 3; 6. 4; 7. 70; 8. 60; 9. 35; 10. 820; 11. 8,000; 12. 19; Students should draw three lines under the first letter of the following words: (paragraph 1): North, America, Easter, Sunday, Florida; (paragraph 2): Florida, King, Phillip; (paragraph 3): Menendez, Florida, American, Indian, Seloy, American, Indians, St. Augustine; Order of answers may vary within classifications but will include: I. Animals; A. vertebrates; 1. mammals; a. cows; b. lions; 2. reptiles; a. snakes; b. crocodiles; 3. amphibians; a. salamanders; b. frogs; 4. birds; a. robins; b. cardinals

Day 14: 1. 6; 2. 0.003; 3. 48; 4. 450; 5. 352; 6. 66; 7. 64; 8. 4,000,000; 9. 147; 10. 7.08; 11. 5; 12. 35,000; 13. 1; 14. 0.5 or $\frac{1}{2}$; 15. Angie tossed broccoli, tomatoes, and cauliflower into her salad; 16. Tyler, if you will help me roll the dough, you can sample some cookies when they are done; 17. Mr. Troute, the counselor at our middle school, forgot that we scheduled an appointment this morning; 18. Before we start the game, we need to read the rules; 19. You will need to bring the hot dogs and buns, and I will bring everything else; 20. Since the weather forecaster predicted rain, the girls decided to change their afternoon plans; 21. N; 22. E; 23. P; 24. nuclear; 25. solar; 26. hydroelectric; 27. wind; 28. geothermal; 29. biomass; 30. gasohol

Day 15: 1. 1,004.8 ft.³; 2. 280 mm³; 3. 80 cm³; 4. 216 m³; 5. 75.40 yd.³; 6. 268.08 m³; 7. When Nathan found a package that was left unattended, he immediately notified airport security;

8. The answer, of course, is yes; 9. In spite of his fear of heights, Richard bought a plane ticket to California yesterday; 10. The Union and Central Pacific Railroads met at Promontory Point, Utah, on May 10, 1869; 11. Mrs. Ancelet, our eighth-grade math teacher, challenges students to perform to the best of their abilities; 12. While Veterans Day is marked by parades and a holiday from work, Americans also should remember the men and women who served and sacrificed for their country; 13. B; 14. A; 15. 1990; 16. C

Day 16: 1. Answers will vary; 2. 4, 5, 6, 7; 3. 4; 4. low: 46, high: 74; 5. 28; 6. P, The answer, of course, is 44; 7. A, Bridget, the tallest girl on the team, is a great tennis player; 8. D, If you wait, Justin, we will go with you; 9. D, Button, stop scratching the cushions; 10. D, Nadia, please call your brother on the phone; 11. D, I told you, Shay, not to wait too long to start your project; 12. A, Mrs. Ramirez, the hardest seventh-grade English teacher, gave me an A on my essay; 13–17. Answers will vary; 18. physical change; 19. chemical change; 20. physical change; 21. physical change; 22. chemical change

Day 17: 1. $\frac{1}{6}$; 2. $\frac{7}{18}$; 3. $\frac{4}{9}$; 4. $\frac{5}{6}$; 5. $\frac{5}{9}$; 6. $\frac{5}{9}$; 7. The weather forecaster on Channel 7 said, "We could have at least two inches of rain tonight."; 8. "The Celebrated Jumping Frog of Calaveras County" is one of Mark Twain's best known short stories.; 9. Anita asked her older brother, "Could I please have a slice of that pizza?"; 10. "No matter how well I prepare for a test," said Jason, "I still get nervous until I can review the test in my hands."; 11. "What a Wonderful World," sung by Louis Armstrong, has long been considered a classic.; 12. "If you practice every day," Coach Bailey said, "you will play better as a team."; 13. glossary; 14. bibliography; 15. index; 16. caption; 17. title page; 18. pictures; 19. table of contents

Day 18: 1. $\frac{1}{6}$; 2. $\frac{1}{3}$; 3. $\frac{1}{2}$; 4. $\frac{5}{6}$; 5. $\frac{1}{2}$; 6. $\frac{2}{3}$; 7. Mr. Cole decided to meet with Ms. Grayson, Ben's math teacher; Mr. Robbins, his science teacher; and Mrs. Abernathy, his English teacher.; 8. Raymond Webb just graduated from college; he plans to attend law school.; 9. The first rule in this class: respect other students' rights.; 10. The parent company left its main facility open but closed plants in Greensboro, North Carolina; Jacksonville, Florida; and Harrisburg, Pennsylvania.; 11. Will Rogers made this comment on attitude: "Don't let yesterday use up too much of today."; 12. Alyson accepted the job as a telemarketer for one reason: she wanted to work at home while Amy was a baby.; 13. Have you ever heard the quote, "You can't afford the luxury of a negative thought"?; 14. Grace did well in three subjects; therefore, she will have a high average at the end of the semester.; 15. C; 16. theater, dance, sculpting, and painting; 17. They had to pass a difficult exam; 18. to determine the empire's population; 19. because new roads and canals made travel easier

Day 19: 1. 36, 34, 41, 10; 2. 15, 14, 14, 22; 3. 16, 10, 10, 27; 4. 42, 41, 41, 66; The origin of the ice-cream cone has been controversial for several centuries. Some historians claim that the first paper cone came from France, while others maintain that metal cones were used in Germany. Still, other people say that an Italian genius introduced the first ice-cream cone.

Ice cream was referred to in Europe as "iced pudding," and the cones were called "wafers." Eating establishments often served the wafers after a meal to soothe digestion. But, once chefs rolled the wafers into funnels, the cones could be filled with anything, including ice cream.

However, many Americans believe that the first edible ice-cream cone was created in the United States. Italo Marchiony, who emigrated

from Italy, created edible cones and sold them from pushcarts in the streets of New York City for a penny each. Marchiony eventually patented his invention in 1903; 5–9. Reasons will vary. 5. A; 6. C; 7. D; 8. B; 9. A

Day 20: 1. 23.8, 19, 19, 18; 2. 17, 16, 12, 21; 3. 25.57, 22, 7, 46; 4. 55.29, 56, 56, 54; 5. B; 6. A; 7. A; 8. A; 9. B; 10. A; 11. B; 12. A;

Ellen (runner)

Julie (skater) **Ben (golfer)**

Dante (tennis player)

13. Johannes Gutenberg; 14. Miguel de Cervantes; 15. Michelangelo; 16. Galileo Galilei; 17. Leonardo da Vinci; 18. John Milton; 19. Nicolaus Copernicus

Erosion: 1. wind; 2. water; 3. ice

Examining the Effects of Acid Rain: Answers will vary; orange juice; vinegar; orange juice; vinegar

Budgeting: Answers will vary.

Comparing Countries: Answers will vary but may include Argentina: 41.77 million (est.); Buenos Aires; Spanish; republic; corn, wheat, livestock, petroleum, or other acceptable products; Finland: 5.26 million (est.); Helsinki; Finnish and Swedish; constitutional republic; barley, fish, metals, timber, or other acceptable products; Cambodia: 14.41 million (est.); Phnom Penh; Khmer; democracy under a constitutional monarchy; sugar, rubber, rice, or other acceptable products.

Reading a Dot Map: 1. bodies of water; 2. Indonesia; 3. Papua New Guinea; 4. Indonesia; 5. Laos and Cambodia; 6. Each dot equals 100,000 people.

accurate	alleged	anticipate
© Carson-Dellosa	© Carson-Dellosa	© Carson-Dellosa
arrogant	assertive	bias
© Carson-Dellosa	© Carson-Dellosa	© Carson-Dellosa
boughs	budget	buoyancy
© Carson-Dellosa	© Carson-Dellosa	© Carson-Dellosa

consistent	debate	deficit
designate	disrupted	dynasty
evoke	exile	extract

flourish	fragile	geyser
© Carson-Dellosa	© Carson-Dellosa	© Carson-Dellosa
haggard	immortalized	indigenous
© Carson-Dellosa	© Carson-Dellosa	© Carson-Dellosa
innovation	intrepid	magma
© Carson-Dellosa	© Carson-Dellosa	© Carson-Dellosa

maxim	mingle	nectar
© Carson-Dellosa	© Carson-Dellosa	© Carson-Dellosa
nimble	obsolete	ominous
© Carson-Dellosa	© Carson-Dellosa	© Carson-Dellosa
omitted	originate	pastoral
© Carson-Dellosa	© Carson-Dellosa	© Carson-Dellosa

phases	phenomena	porous
© Carson-Dellosa	© Carson-Dellosa	© Carson-Dellosa
proclamation	quench	radiant
© Carson-Dellosa	© Carson-Dellosa	© Carson-Dellosa
retrieved	sabotage	sediment
© Carson-Dellosa	© Carson-Dellosa	© Carson-Dellosa

segregated	sulk	teeming
© Carson-Dellosa	© Carson-Dellosa	© Carson-Dellosa
terrain	thrifty	unison
© Carson-Dellosa	© Carson-Dellosa	© Carson-Dellosa
valiant	verge	wrench
© Carson-Dellosa	© Carson-Dellosa	© Carson-Dellosa

$14 + (3 \times 5)$	$72 \div (24 \div 3)$	$(12 \div 3) \times 9$
$3(6 \times 2)$	$7(63 \div 9)$	$5(14 - 3)$
$(-7)(-2)$	$-4 \times (-2)$	$49 \div (-7)$

$-36 \div 9$	-4×4	$-63 \div (-6)$
© Carson-Dellosa	© Carson-Dellosa	© Carson-Dellosa
$-44 \div (-11)$	$4 \times (-5)$	$56 \div (-8)$
© Carson-Dellosa	© Carson-Dellosa	© Carson-Dellosa
$(5)(-7)$	$24 \div (-6)$	$-15 \div 5$
© Carson-Dellosa	© Carson-Dellosa	© Carson-Dellosa

-12×6	$(-11)(10)$	$-36 \div (-12)$
© Carson-Dellosa	© Carson-Dellosa	© Carson-Dellosa
$(5)(-12)$	$5 + 3 \times 4$	$14 \div 2 \times 6$
© Carson-Dellosa	© Carson-Dellosa	© Carson-Dellosa
$11 - 3 + 5$	$3(5 + 4)$	$24 \div 6 - 2$
© Carson-Dellosa	© Carson-Dellosa	© Carson-Dellosa

$8 + 6 \div 3$

$3 \cdot 5 - 4 \cdot 8$

$12 - 49 \div 7$

$7 + 2 \cdot 2$

$21 \div (2 + 5)$

$15 \div 5 \cdot 2$

$(-6) - (-6) =$

$(-4) + (-3) =$

$-11 - (-5)$

$b - 10 = 43$

© Carson-Dellosa

$f + 3 = 12$

© Carson-Dellosa

$9 + p = 9$

© Carson-Dellosa

$7 = 15 + k$

© Carson-Dellosa

$h + 5 = -16$

© Carson-Dellosa

$-3 = m + 5$

© Carson-Dellosa

$15 = 33 - y$

© Carson-Dellosa

$v \cdot 4 = 20$

© Carson-Dellosa

$36 \div c = 4$

© Carson-Dellosa

$5 + r = 17$

$81 = 9 \cdot v$

$56 \div z = 8$

$k \cdot 2 = 22$

$11 + t = 45$

$39 = j \cdot 2$

$4 \cdot x = 60$

$75 \div n = 3$

$20 \cdot w = 120$

$$\frac{3}{4}$$

$$\frac{6}{10}$$

$$\frac{1}{5}$$

$$\frac{1}{4}$$

$$\frac{3}{10}$$

$$\frac{23}{40}$$

$$\frac{7}{1000}$$

$$\frac{36}{100}$$

$$\frac{12}{15}$$

0.2	0.6	0.75
© Carson-Dellosa	© Carson-Dellosa	© Carson-Dellosa
0.575	0.3	0.25
© Carson-Dellosa	© Carson-Dellosa	© Carson-Dellosa
0.8	0.36	0.007
© Carson-Dellosa	© Carson-Dellosa	© Carson-Dellosa